Getting Started with Passive Income

Getting Started with

Passive Income

Steve Pavlina

WAKING LION PRESS

ISBN 978-1-4341-0565-3

Published by Waking Lion Press, an imprint of the Editorium

Waking Lion Press™ and Editorium™ are trademarks of:

The Editorium, LLC
West Jordan, UT 84081-6132
www.editorium.com

Contents

v

Introduction

Passive income is money that comes to you even when you're not actively working, such as royalties, investment income, and revenue from automated business systems.

I started earning passive income in the 1990s by creating, selling, and licensing computer games. Once those deals and systems were established, I continued to earn money from those products year after year.

This approach soon became a habit. Consequently, most of the money I've earned during my lifetime has come from passive or semi-passive income source, not from a salary, wage, or hourly rate.

It took me many years to figure out how to make a living this way, and I went bankrupt along the way, but eventually I learned what I needed to learn. It works, and I definitely appreciate the benefits of it.

The truth is that it's much, much easier to earn passive income today than it was when I first began on this path. There are such ridiculous opportunities out there, especially online, that if you're at least halfway intelligent, you can surely do this. There are ways to earn money online now where you don't even need your own website, nor do you need to have a lot of money to start earning passive income.

Earning passive income is not difficult. The how-to part — the actual doing of it — is fairly straightforward.

The difficult part is wrapping your head around it, unloading a lot of false conditioning, maintaining a constructive mindset, and shedding illogical fears. The challenge here is your own self development . . . to grow into the man or woman who won't block themselves from doing this.

First I'll share some ideas to help you understand the right mindset for earning passive income. People have a lot of B.S. beliefs in their heads with respect to earning income, and I want to squash some of them (the beliefs, that is, not their heads), so they don't get in our way later. This part may be more emotional than logical, but the truth is that the motivation to earn any kind of income is largely emotional, and we need to address that. There's no logical mandate to earn income; it may feel like it's essential for survival, but our species supposedly managed without money for most of its existence.

Then I'll share a great deal of how-to information. Some of this will be fairly general, so it can be applied to all forms of passive income. But I'll also give you more detailed how-to info for the forms of passive income that I'm most familiar with, which is mostly going to be in the online realm.

I can't teach you real estate or stock investing, nor can I teach you how to create a blog as successful as mine has been. But I can still teach you how to create your own streams of passive income, first in a general way and then specifically in the methods I've used.

I'll do my best to make this easy for you to follow, so you'll be able to create a stream of income without needing to spend a lot of money, and I'll make it so you don't even need a website either. Obviously my website gives me a major marketing advantage, so I'll share how to do the marketing aspect if you're starting from scratch. I want to make it so that even a high school student working from home in his/her spare time could go through this process with me.

I'm also going to maintain a very moderate pacing here, so you can follow along in real time without needing to work on this full time to keep up.

If you want to read this book just for educational or for entertainment purposes, that's fine. But I'm really not writing this for the casual dabbler or the wannabe. I'm doing this for those who'd really want to get started on this path now. Consequently, we're going to take it nice and slow and build a solid foundation. I'm not just going to throw a bunch of information at you and hope you make sense of it.

If you simply follow these steps with me, including getting into the passive income mindset, then this year you're going to create at least one new stream of passive income for yourself. This book will focus on helping you create that specific result. If that's a result you want, then we're on the same page.

I'm undoubtedly going to weave personal growth lessons into this material because passive income ties in with personal growth in such amazing ways, especially with respect to setting and achieving goals, self-discipline, and overcoming limiting beliefs.

Logically this is an achievable goal. It's not like we're trying to figure out how to mine space asteroids. People figured out how to earn passive income thousands of years ago. Surely with all the additional knowledge and resources available to you today, you can do this too.

Chapter 1

What Is Passive Income?

I want to kick off this book by clarifying what I mean by passive income.

I prefer to define passive income fairly broadly as revenue you earn even when you aren't actively working. Another name for passive income is *residual income*.

By contrast *active income* is money that stops coming to you when you stop working. If you get paid a salary and you quit your job or get laid off, most likely you'll stop getting paid. You may get a severance package to help you transition, but your boss won't keep paying your salary unless you keep showing up for work.

Similarly, if you do contract work for clients who pay you, and if you'll stop getting paid if you stop doing this work, that's also active income. You may have more flexibility with contract work, but you still have to do the work to receive your payments.

With passive income, you would keep getting paid whether or not you do any meaningful work. You may do a lot of work up front to get the ball rolling, but eventually you reach a point where the passive income stream gets activated. At this point you can essentially stop working on this income stream if you so desire, and more money will keep flowing to you through this stream regardless what you do or don't do.

Passive income doesn't mean one-time lump sum payments such as an inheritance or the sale of an asset like your home or some stock you own. Passive income is a source of income with some sense of continuation over time.

Passive income doesn't mean permanent income. Some forms of passive income may last a few years. Other forms may keep going for decades or even for centuries across multiple generations. But all forms of income eventually dry up for one reason or another.

Passive income doesn't mean 100% secure income. As Helen Keller wrote, "Security is mostly a superstition." Some forms of income are more secure than others, but there's always a risk element. For any income source, there's a non-zero probability that something could destroy it. This is one reason it's often wise to create multiple streams of income, so you can reduce the risk that all of them will fail simultaneously.

Passive income doesn't mean perfectly 100% passive with no maintenance required. With any income source, you may need to do a little maintenance to keep it going. Sometimes this is really easy and only involves checking your mail and depositing checks. Sometimes it's even more passive when the money is deposited directly into your bank account every month. But then you may still need to report this income and pay taxes on it.

Passive income is really a spectrum of possibilities. Some income streams are very passive. If you do essentially no maintenance on them for years, the income will keep coming. My book royalties are one example of this. Regardless of what I do or don't do, most likely Hay House will keep selling my book, *Personal Development for Smart People*, and people will keep buying it:

https://stevepavlina.com/personal-development-for-smart-people/

Even if I shut down my website and go incognito for some reason, my book can keep selling online and in bookstores. All I need to do is deposit the royalty checks. I don't have to process orders, interact with customers, or do any ongoing marketing.

Other income streams are semi-passive. You may need to do some work to maintain them even if you're not working for a salary. For example, if you own a house and rent it out, you may earn passive income as rent payments from your tenants. But you may also need to invest some time, energy, and money to maintain the property, to find new tenants when the place goes vacant, and to handle the mortgage, insurance payments, and property taxes. If your tenants get ornery or become delinquent, you may need to do even more work. You may delegate much of this work to someone else, but then you have a business partner or employee to manage instead.

Passive income doesn't mean it's passive for everyone. There may be other people with regular jobs who do some of the work that enables you to receive passive income. You may also leverage technology to do a lot of work for you. The level of passivity is perspective dependent. One person's passive income is another person's active income.

I also want to distinguish passive income from what I'll call *moocher income*. Moocher income is what people try to earn when they succumb to a get-rich-quick mindset. This is an undisciplined attitude that seeks to get something for nothing. The idea is to find a way to mooch money from people or the economy without providing any meaningful value. It is possible to generate income this way since markets contain plenty of inefficiencies, but it's not an approach I recommend. I don't personally define passive income to include moocher income, but there is a spectrum here where some forms of passive income deliver more value than others.

In this book I intend to help you create passive income in a way that generates good value for others. This is more sustainable in the long run, and it's better for everyone. Fortunately there are lots of ways to create value.

That said, this isn't a book for the lazy-ass delusional types who spend six hours a day playing Angry Farm Ninja Madness. Nor is it intended for the desperate "I need to make $500 by Friday to pay my rent" nutters. Creating passive income streams is work. You can meditate on abundance, invoke the Law of Attraction, and pray to Hestia all you want, but also expect to do some real work if you're going to make passive income a reality for you. Creating streams of passive income is a very active endeavor. You must do the work first; then you can enjoy the results.

P.S. If you do wish to pray for assistance, don't pray to Hestia unless you want a baby or need to start a fire. Pray to Hades (aka Pluto) since he's the god of wealth.

Just don't tell Hestia.

Chapter 2

The End Game of Passive Income

Let's talk about the reality of what it's like to create streams of passive income and how it compares to working at a regular job. What I'll share here may surprise you.

With a typical job, you're more or less directly trading your working hours for dollars. You may receive an hourly wage, a salary, and/or bonuses for the time you put in at work. Your ongoing pay depends on your continued presence at work. If you stop working, your paycheck stops as well.

With passive income you'll often get paid nothing at first. Initially you work to create and/or leverage a system that generates a flow of income long-term. Once your new income stream is launched and the *passive* phase begins, you may not have to work very much at all beyond that to maintain the stream.

Passive income is one strategy among many for earning money. It doesn't necessarily dictate any particular choice of careers. You can do many different types of work and use passive income strategies to monetize your work.

Passive vs. Active Income

Suppose you're a writer. One way to earn active income would be to get a job writing for a magazine or newspaper. You could get paid to write articles which your employer publishes and owns. You would receive a wage from your employer for the service you provide. If you stop writing in this scenario, you'll stop getting paid.

Now suppose you offer your writing skills as an independent contractor. You market and sell your services to people and businesses. You do this on a "work for hire" basis, getting paid for each job you complete. This is also active income. If you stop working, your income ceases.

Now suppose you write a book and sign a publishing deal with a book publisher. The publisher gets your book into bookstores and also sells it online. They send you royalty checks twice a year based on sales of the book. You receive a percentage of what they receive for every copy sold. Five years later you're still receiving checks from them. Your royalties are passive income. Even if you stop working after your book is published, you'll continue to receive royalty payments for the book that did get published. You could potentially continue to receive these payments for the rest of your life. Your book may eventually be purchased by people who aren't even born yet.

Notice that in each scenario, your underlying career is essentially the same. You're still the same writer. You're just using different strategies for earning income. You could even apply all three strategies simultaneously, working at a regular job, doing contract work on the side, and also writing a book and getting it published.

At any time you're free to use active income, passive income, or hybrid strategies — or any combo of these you wish. You don't have to quit your active income job to set up streams of passive income. For some people this is easier, however, since a regular job can chew up a lot of time, making it harder to find the time to create passive income.

Sometimes you can even get paid to create your streams of passive income. For instance, our writer may receive an advance for his/her book from the publisher. So not only does this writer earn long-term passive income, but s/he also gets paid to set it up.

Where Does Passive Income Lead?

I want you to start thinking about how your life would be impacted if you took the time to create some streams of passive income. Suppose you succeed. What then?

What would your life be like if you were receiving an extra $100 per month in passive income? What about an extra $500? $2500? $10K? 50K?

At what point do you shift from *That wouldn't make much difference* to *That would be nice*? Then when do you think, *That would really take off some pressure*?

What amount nudges you into *I could live off of that amount*? Then when do you think, *Wow, I could really upgrade my lifestyle with that*?

And if you want to think beyond that, where do you start thinking, *Hmmm. I wonder what I'd do if I earned that much without having to do anything? What would I actually do with my time then?*

It may surprise you that one of the reasons people avoid earning passive income is the fear that arises from being confronted with that last question. People often spend so much of their lives distracted by the daily grind of work, bills, and social obligations that they rarely give much thought to the bigger questions. Suppose you actually do succeed here in a big way? Then what?

If your end game looks bleak, empty, and meaningless, that's going to hold you back. You'll sabotage yourself before you get very far.

Will Passive Income Make You a Bigger Success or a Bigger Failure?

If you didn't have to work and money kept flowing to you month after month, what would you do with your time? Would you play video games all day or do drugs or sit around watching TV and eating?

I actually found it pretty difficult to succeed in creating passive income until I was able to answer these questions seriously. My answer changes from time to time, but the core is that I want to spend my life growing, creating, and sharing. I want to keep adding something of value to the substance of the universe. Whenever I keep doing that, regardless of how much money I'm making, I feel happy and fulfilled.

The irony is that if you answer this question honestly, you'll probably come up with something that you could just as easily do when you're broke, although perhaps not at the same level.

Because of my passive income streams, I can afford to be really lazy if I wanted to. I could sit around doing nothing for weeks on end, and my bills would still be covered. For some people this may sound like paradise, but it presents its own challenges. If you're not careful, you could easily slide into a serious depression in this kind of situation. People receive a lot of fulfillment from work, but if you no longer have to work, will you still be able to motivate yourself to tackle new challenges, or will you do little or nothing because you can?

Many people have created passive income streams that cover all their expenses, and they ended up depressed and listless. Some try to keep the treadmill going by creating even more passive income streams, but their hearts just aren't in it, and they eventually burn out.

What's Your Motivation?

When I was broke and deep in debt and about to declare bankruptcy, I asked myself what I'd want to do with my life if I knew for certain that I'd *always* be broke. That was an interesting question because it helped me get past the momentary distractions of money and bills that always seemed to be at the urgent forefront of my reality. I realized that what I really wanted to do with my time was to create and share. I noticed this was something I could always do in some fashion regardless of how much money I had. This shift in mindset allowed me to increase my happiness and fulfillment, not to mention turning around my financial life, in less than a year.

This mindset also helped motivate me to create passive income streams because the more I did that, the more I got material distractions out of the way, and the more time I had for creative projects.

My life flows nicely when I remember to use my time for creative endeavors like writing, speaking, and creating workshops. It doesn't flow so well when I allow myself to feel like I'm swimming in time with nothing meaningful to do.

It may seem premature to think about this now, but I think

it's pretty important. If deep down you know that the end game of creating passive income is going to be a bust for you — that you'll just end up living like a big loser day after day — then will you really be motivated to get there? That would probably require a lot of pushing and force to get yourself to take action.

If, on the other hand, you can envision a pleasant and fulfilling end game scenario, I think it will be much easier to create passive income streams in a more peaceful and flowing way. There will still be work to do, but at least you won't be internally fighting yourself along the way.

If anything stops you from earning passive income, what will it be? It's undoubtedly going to be something inside you. The external action steps are certainly doable. You may screw things up in the beginning — I sure did! — but if you persist and learn from your mistakes, it's largely a done deal that you'll succeed. As I mentioned in a previous post, people were earning passive income thousands of years ago. Surely you can learn this as well. So the only thing that's really capable of stopping you here is you.

Beyond the Hype

I know there's a lot of hype around passive income. Yes, it's cool. Yes, it can relieve a lot of financial pressure. Yes, it can make a big difference in your lifestyle. I must say that a lot of the hype is true. As Earl Nightingale said, "Nothing can take the place of money in the area in which money works."

But suppose you really get there. Suppose you cover all your expenses and then some with passive income. Then what? What will you do with your time? And will you be truly happy doing that, year after year and decade after decade? Or will you feel even more lost than you do now?

Here's what I suggest. Write down a little vision statement for yourself, perhaps a few sentences or a paragraph about how you'd choose to live if all of your expenses were covered by passive income, and you didn't actually have to work to pay the bills.

Then set that statement aside, and look at it tomorrow fresh. Now ask yourself if you'd really be happy in this scenario. If you don't think you'd be very happy there, rewrite your statement. Try to get clear about what your personal end game of passive income looks like. See if you can create a scenario in which you're very happy.

Finally, if you aren't already doing what you wrote in your vision statement now, then why not? Could you still do it in some capacity under your current conditions if you really wanted to?

Money is Fuel, Not a Cure

You see, if you're holding yourself back now, then why wouldn't you continue to hold yourself back even after you've created your abundant passive income streams? If you allow yourself to use lack of money as an excuse today, you're just going to use a different excuse when you have more financial abundance. Money is no cure for the willingness to succumb to feeble excuses. So if you see this pattern in yourself, then I suggest you start working to overcome it today.

Money is more multiplicative than transformative in its effects. It makes you more of who you already are. So if you're the kind of person who will excuse yourself from a bigger vision today, adding more money to this situation will only make things worse. Many people who have lots of money also have many more obligations to use as excuses. The excuse making doesn't end with more money; it only magnifies.

It may seem like having lots of free time to play is a great thing, but a playboy/playgirl lifestyle probably won't create much fulfillment. More people seem to find fulfillment in meaningful work. Yes, you can still play and travel and all that good stuff. But give some thought to what work you might wish to pursue if you didn't have to work for money at all. This is an important question to answer. Equally important is to ask: *Why aren't you doing this work right now in some fashion?*

I personally feel that the #1 benefit of having my expenses covered by passive income is that I get to keep doing a lot more of the kind of work I enjoy. I also get to work the way I want to work — where I want, when I want, how I want, and with whom I want. But in order to maintain those feelings of fulfillment and meaning in my life, the work must continue. I can't just go into perpetual play mode and check out.

I think you'll find that if you're already living your bigger vision in some capacity, then creating streams of passive income will be a lot easier. These streams will help you expand your vision and overcome distractions.

But if you're currently using feeble excuses like the lack of money, lack of time, or the obligations of your day job to distract you from a bigger vision — even as you somehow still have time for Facebook, texting, email, reading blogs, watching TV, etc. — then I'd bet that you're not going to succeed in creating much passive income; you're the type who will come up with an excuse to quit, and even reading this is just another distraction for you.

So whatever it is that you think you might start doing once you're already living the dream of total financial abundance, start doing that now in some fashion. Insert it into your life, even if it's just for a couple hours a week to start. If you don't have time for it, quit Facebook, give up TV, and cancel your texting plan.

Chapter 3

Set Your Passive Income Goal

As we transition into the how-to aspect of passive income creation, let's begin by having you set a goal for what you want to accomplish here.

Why are you reading this? Is it just for entertainment's sake? Do you hope to learn something that you might apply later? Or do you actually want to create at least one new stream of passive income this year?

Let me suggest a simple meta-goal for starters: By the time you're done reading this chapter, set a clear goal for what you want to gain from this book.

Do not move on to something else until you've set a clear and specific passive income goal.

No feeble excuses. No vacillating. No "I'll think about it later" B.S. And please no lame-ass "I want more money" vague answers.

Whatever excuse you come up with as to why you can't set a clear goal right now, we both know it's stupid, so let's not even go there. Not setting a goal is a waste of time.

If your actual desire is to create a new stream of passive income, then let's make sure your goal includes 3 aspects:

1. how much money you want to earn per month from your next stream of passive income (specific dollar amount)

2. how long you expect that stream to last (number of years)

3. your deadline for receiving your first month's income from that stream

This isn't your ultimate goal we're talking about here. It's the goal for your first (or your next, if you've done this before) stream of passive income.

If you have something different in mind that doesn't really fit the parameters above, then by all means set the goal you feel is best for you. At the end of the year, when other people are enjoying their new streams of passive income, you can see how your own goal worked out.

The idea is to set a goal that's *motivating* but that's also *believable* for you.

If you're telling yourself that you can't earn any passive income because it's too much for you, then your imagination needs work. You could put $100 in a free savings account and earn a trickle of passive income each year for decades. So don't be lazy here. Don't let yourself off the hook. Set a goal.

Goal setting is a skill that takes practice. If you fumble this initially and set a goal that's too big and unbelievable for you, you won't achieve it. If you set an unrealistic deadline, you'll blow the deadline. How do you know what's realistic? You learn with practice, just like you learned to walk and talk.

I don't expect your goal to be perfect. That isn't the point. The goal is just the first step to get you moving forward and taking this seriously. The ultimate goal is to get good at setting and achieving your goals. This means you have to risk making mistakes in the beginning.

As the saying goes, *There never was a winner who wasn't at some point a beginner.* So begin by setting a goal.

My First Passive Income Streams

Other than earning interest on my savings account, my first real experience with long-term passive income was when I wrote and self-published a computer game for MS-Windows. I think I released it in 1995. It was a simple side-scrolling shoot-em-up game. I did the programming and artwork for it myself (I wasn't much of an artist, though), and my girlfriend at the time did the music and helped out with the sound effects.

The game didn't sell particularly well. I put it up on my website, but my website had virtually no traffic. I also uploaded it to a bunch of free download software sites. I had a free demo with a couple of levels, and then people would get more levels if they bought the full version. Initially most of my sales came from people finding the demo on a game download site, and the demo would refer them to my website to buy the game.

I opened a Post Office box and started receiving mail orders for the game. Later I got a merchant account, so I could take credit card orders. Then I started accepting online orders. Eventually I set things up so that orders could be processed and fulfilled automatically.

On average I earned about $75 per month from this game. I didn't do much in terms of marketing, other than posting it on my website and submitting it to those download sites, which was a one-time effort. Once the game started selling, I moved on to other projects.

This was a Windows 3. 1 game with a fixed 640×480 resolution. It was strictly 2D, so there were no fancy 3D graphics or anything like that.

A year after I released it, the game was still earning about $75 per month.

Five years after its release, it was still earning about the same.

Ten years after its release, it was still earning about the same.

I varied the price of the game over the years, testing $9. 95, $14. 95, and $19. 95. It earned roughly the same amount of money regardless of the price. I could sell 10 copies for $10 each or 5 copies for $20 each.

The game was initially available on 3. 5 diskettes, then on CD-ROM. More than 90% of the customers bought the instant download version.

I also did some licensing deals for this game with LCR publishers (LCR = low cost retail). These publishers found me as a result of finding my game on some download site. They'd put together collections of cheap games and sell them on CDs for under $10. I didn't earn much money from these deals, but they gave my game wider distribution, and every copy included a link to my website.

Occasionally the game got some special attention, and there was a surge in sales where it might do double sales for a month. So overall it probably earned in the range of $10–15K over its lifetime.

It took me about 6 months to write and release this game. I had a lot to learn, so it was slow going. I got much faster as I learned and practiced. Writing a similar shoot-em-up game in 1998 only took me about 2 weeks, including the design, programming, artwork, and sound effects.

Eventually I released three more games at about the same level of quality. And again, each of these added another $75 per month in passive income, so with 4 of these titles, I was up to $300 per month.

Finally I got smart and spent 6 months creating a much better game and put more effort into marketing it. It did $500 in sales its first month and was up to $2K per month a few months later. I kept building it up from there with two expansion packs and a deluxe version that sold for $24. 95. The game did very well and dwarfed the results of my previous games. I also did more licensing deals for it, including one that had a minimum guarantee of $5K per month just from that one source.

I developed this hit game with a $0 budget. I did the design and programming, and the artist worked for a percentage of royalties, so I created a passive income stream for him.

Then I went on to license and republish games from other developers, which created new passive income streams for them and me. Eventually I built up a suite of about two dozen games, which means two dozen streams of mostly passive income. Some streams were pretty good. Others were just a trickle.

In 2006 I finally took my games off the market when I shut down my games business. By this point I was earning so much more from StevePavlina.com that I didn't want to divide my focus by keeping my games business going. But the passive income stream from these games helped me launch my personal growth business. My games income covered all my expenses while I got StevePavlina.com up and running.

Taking the Long View

Is $10K spread out over 10 years a good paycheck for 6 months of work? No, I could easily have earned more money working at a job. I was already earning more than that from contract programming work before I wrote my first independent game.

The point of creating your first passive income stream isn't to achieve that big payout right away. The point is to *learn how* to create passive income streams, so you can get better at it. Then you can create bigger streams as your skills increase. Don't expect your first effort to be your masterpiece.

Today I can create new streams of passive income with a lot less effort than I had to exert in the 1990s. The reason I can do this is because I put in the time to learn how to do this, and I've continued to refine my skills over time.

Don't worry about how big your streams are in the beginning. If you can create a $50 per month passive income stream this year, I think that's great. And it's so much easier to do this today than it was back in 1995 when I first started, so you have it much easier than I did. Your cell phone is probably 100 times more powerful than the computer I used back then.

You also have me coaching you along the way. I didn't have anyone coaching me at the time. Sometimes the people in my life suggested that I should get a job. They don't say that anymore though.

Do set goals, but be patient with your progress. This is a skill that will benefit you your whole life. Even if you work on this for 10 years, there will still be plenty more to learn.

My Passive Income Goal

As part of this book, I'll walk you through the process of creating a new stream of passive income. And while writing this material, I created a new stream for myself in the process. I hadn't decided what that would be yet, but I was sure I'd come up with something. Coming up with ideas is easy.

But the goal has to come first. Since I wanted to keep this simple and not overcomplicate things, I set what is for me a relatively conservative goal:

I create a new stream of passive income by September 30, 2012, that generates at least $2,000 per month on average and endures for a minimum of 10 years.

So that meant creating a new stream that earned at least $240,000 over the next decade.

This seemed like an achievable goal for me. I've already created multiple streams of this size and larger, so it wasn't a stretch to believe that I could do it again. In this case the challenge was to explain all the steps as I go along, which I'd never done before. I wanted to keep this goal fairly basic so I could focus on the teaching aspect.

Having a clear and specific goal helped me transition to thinking about the how, so I could start pondering ways to do this.

That also helped me rule out what I *couldn't* do to create that income stream. I couldn't just do more public workshops or paid speaking since that's active income. I wanted to set something up once and have it generate monthly income for at least a decade.

What would happen if I didn't make the deadline? Nothing. I'd set a *new* deadline. The deadline is a focusing mechanism. I could create a new passive income stream within a couple of weeks if I wanted to. But for this stream, I wanted to take it slow and explain the process in detail, so you could follow along. But I also wanted to keep moving towards some kind of release. I didn't want to get stuck in perpetual idea mode.

Your Passive Income Goal

The key to goal setting is to get into the habit of *setting and achieving goals*. It's not to set aggressive targets that you never reach. You can always set a bigger goal later once you achieve the original goal.

Sometimes I've set a big goal with a 2-month deadline, and I achieved it during the first week or two. So I celebrated that. Then I set a new goal with a new deadline.

As long as the goal seems motivating to you and it helps you get into action, then I'd say it a good goal for you.

My suggestion would be to set a goal something like this:

I create a new stream of passive income this year that generates at least $100 per month on average and endures for a minimum of 5 years.

I think this is a very achievable goal for most people. You don't need your own website to earn this much.

Now some people will blow this goal out of the water; it will be way too easy for them. Other people will find it a serious challenge. Feel free to adjust the goal to something that feels good to you.

If you were to achieve the goal above, you'd put at least $6K in your pocket, but it's not the amount that matters. The real aim is for you to learn how to create a $100 per month stream of passive income. Once you learn how to do that, you can surely do it again. Do it 10 times, and you'll earn $60K passively.

Once you learn how to earn $100 per month in passive income — by actually doing it, not by reading about it — then it's not that difficult to learn to create bigger streams. So instead of creating 10 streams that collectively generate $60K, you might learn how to earn that much with just one or two streams. As you continue to develop your skills in this area, you'll discover how to earn larger sums with fewer streams and less effort. If one stream dies, you'll also know how to replace it with a new one.

I'm pretty comfortable creating streams that earn around $50K per year. When I had third-party ads on my website several years ago, one of those streams was earning more than $100K per year. Once you get the hang of this, I think you'll find it a fun challenge to create new streams of income and to experiment with different approaches.

If you want more long-term financial security, you won't find it in the money or even in the streams of passive income. You'll find it in building your own knowledge and skills. You can take away all my streams of income, my website, my assets, etc, and I'll be able to recreate the same level of financial abundance in a relatively short period of time because I already know how to do it.

This is what I want for you as well. I want you to learn how to do this, so then you'll always have that option available. This know-how will relieve you of much financial pressure. You won't have to scramble to get a job to pay your bills. You can just create more passive income streams if you want more money.

Do It Now

You are *not* finished reading this chapter until you've set your goal and written it down. If you haven't done this yet, do it right now.

Once you've done that, I encourage you to also post your goal in public — *if* you can do that in a place where you feel that people will support and encourage you.

If you expect mostly positive support, then share your goal on your blog, your Facebook page, etc. Add some accountability and commitment. This can help motivate you to succeed, and you'll inspire others to develop this skill too.

If, on the other hand, you anticipate a largely negative response if you share your goal publicly, then you have a different challenge to address. This means your life is filled with too many incompatible people. You have too much social drag. These people are only going to get in your way, so if you don't think you can win them over, then drop them. Block them, unfriend them, etc.

If other people have a problem with your setting a goal in this area, what are they going to be like when you actually succeed? They'll probably get worse, and then you'll have to deal with problems like pettiness, jealousy, sarcasm, neediness, and more. Better to cut them out now and fill your life with positive support. Let them learn from your example . . . from a distance.

Prepare to succeed. Expect to succeed. Know that once you've set this goal, you're going to achieve it. And if you're going to achieve it, then you need to start shedding from your life whatever would otherwise get in the way of your goal. Whoever can't handle it, drop them. This will create space to invite much better relationships with people who will support you on this path. The dead weight must be shed, so that positive support can come through.

Chapter 4

Commit to Your Passive Income Goal

Now that you've set a specific passive income goal, it's time to strengthen your connection to this goal.

The idea here is to begin believing in your goal so that it becomes more real and solid, not just some airy-fairy fantasy.

Put Your Goal in Your Face

Try this for starters. Grab a piece of paper, write your goal on the paper in a positive, personal, present tense format, and then post this piece of paper somewhere that you'll see it every day, such as on your living room wall or your bathroom mirror. You can even post it in multiple locations if you like.

Based on my goal from the previous chapter, I came up with the following goal/intention statement:

I am now successfully creating a new stream of passive income by September 30, 2012, that generates at least $2,000 per month on average and endures for a minimum of 10 years, and I'm doing this in a way that delivers strong value for many others around the world.

To make my goal more real and concrete, I copied and pasted

the text above into a blank document, increased the font size to fill up the page (46 points in this case), and printed it out in landscape view. Then I tacked it up on the corkboard in my home office. Now whenever I sit at my desk, I can't help but see this goal, since the paper is within my field of view. Even if I don't acknowledge it consciously, my subconscious mind will be exposed to this goal repeatedly. I will keep the paper there (or use some other goal reminder) until this goal is achieved.

Feel free to embellish your goal with language you find attractive. I find it more motivating to set goals that provide value for others, so I added that phrase to the end of my goal.

This step is important because the natural tendency after setting a new goal is to drop the ball very quickly. Many people lose sight of their new goals within a week after setting them. They get sucked into various distractions, and the goal doesn't take root. To prevent your goal from fizzling out, you have to keep giving it some attention, just as you would keep watering a plant.

Create Consequences for Failure

Another thing you can do to make your goal more solid is to create consequences for dropping the ball. Since I'm writing about this along the way, it will be difficult for me to lose sight of this goal. If I quit or flub this up, there will be some negative consequences: Humiliations galore and that sort of thing.

If there's no negative consequence for quitting, it will be easy for you to quit. That's bad. We want to create more resistance to quitting, so that once you get going, it's hard to turn back.

How you do this is a very personal choice, but if you're not willing to do anything of the sort, then how committed are you really? If you're committed to your goal, then it shouldn't be a big deal to line up some extra sting for failure.

Quite often people will find the avoidance of the negative consequences more motivating than the positive benefits they'll achieve. Instead of winning, some people become more focused when they really want to avoid losing. If the positive motivation for passive income was enough for you, wouldn't you have already achieved your goal by now? You could have done this a year ago, such as by using the SBI service that I've been recommending for years:

https://stevepavlina.com/site-build-it/

If you've been interested in this goal for a while but you've been putting it off and you're now telling yourself that you're finally going to do it and that this time things will be different, why should anyone believe you? Do you even believe you? Or are you just trying to act confidently to convince yourself?

If the only consequence of failure is that you continue to experience more of your old reality, that isn't much of a consequence, is it? After all, you're already tolerating that kind of reality right now, so there's no reason to believe you can't keep right on dealing with it for another decade. But if turning back somehow looks nastier than going forward, you'll very likely make some serious progress this time.

One suggestion is to find your biggest doubter and make a bet with him/her that you'll succeed in achieving your goal by the deadline. If they're willing to bet against you, this can engage your competitive spirit and boost your motivation significantly. And if they refuse to bet, it can give more confidence since maybe it means they believe you'll succeed. You can bet money, or you can make the consequences something more creative.

If you're into politics, another idea is to promise to donate money to a candidate or political party that you hate if you don't achieve your goal by the stated deadline.

Your ability to do this is partly a test of how confident you are in achieving your goal. If you struggle to make this sort of commitment, then what does it say about your level of confidence? If you're truly going to achieve your goal, then the negative outcome will not happen.

When you do this, be careful not to create too much of a counter-force to your goal by mistake. You want to engage your competitive spirit if you find that helpful, but you don't want to go so far as to incentivize others to sabotage your success. So if you promise a nice benefit to a bunch of people if you fail, you may motivate people to root for your failure and to withhold help they might otherwise have offered.

Involve Others

One more way to increase your commitment to your goal is to involve others in its achievement. Instead of engaging your competitive spirit, you can create a spirit of cooperation and teamwork.

I believe that we can all achieve our goals together and help and support each other along the way, so I wish to create a spirit of cooperation. I wouldn't find it helpful to have people wishing for me to fail. I'd rather see all of us intending each others' success as well as our individual success.

By creating and sharing a public series of blog posts on how to create passive income, I engaged other people in the achievement of my goal. A positive side effect is that I created a resource to help others achieve similar goals. People generally appreciate this sort of thing, and I've seen a lot of positive feedback. I do appreciate the encouragement, which is very motivating to me.

If I had done this as a private pursuit, I might have found it harder to achieve my goal since I'm the only one who cared about it. But by doing it in a way that invites more social support, it became easier. Yes, it's more work to publicly share the steps along the way, but it also turns a solo project into a social one, which makes it more fun to work on. I also had more accountability to keep moving this project forward week after week.

While thinking about all this, I took a mini-vacation that included a trip to Disneyland, and I didn't do any blogging during that time. But I saw people posting on Twitter that they were looking forward to my next post in the series. By announcing the series publicly, I invited others to hold me accountable and make sure I keep it going. I'm always free to take mini-vacations when I want, but other people nudged me to move this along since they were motivated to receive the value from it. I believe this makes it harder for me to fail. Making it harder to fail means making it more likely to succeed.

If you look at my situation and how I set this up, you'll probably agree that I had some good motivation to complete this series and achieve my goal. Time will be the ultimate judge of course, but in the meantime, have you set up your goal with a similar amount of motivation and pressure? If not, this is the time to make those adjustments. If it's too easy for you to drop the ball, you probably will. I've actually won money betting against people when I could see that they weren't putting enough pressure on themselves to succeed.

Create Positive Stress

We know that too much stress is a bad thing. But we also know that too little stress is bad as well. There's a sweet spot of stress between the extremes where you'll feel motivated to take action. This positive form of stress is called *eustress*.

How else can you strengthen your commitment to your goal? How can you keep it in front of you? How can you make it more real and solid? How can you add more negative consequences for failure? Whatever ideas you come up with, act on them right away. It's okay to be a bit impulsive here. As you do this more and more, you'll learn what works best for you.

It often takes time for a new goal to sink in, so I encourage you to take this step seriously. This is not a difficult step. Creating and posting my goal reminder in my office only took a few minutes. You can do a lot with a short status update on your favorite social media site, such as by promising a negative consequence if you fail to achieve your goal by your deadline.

Surely you can spare a few minutes to strengthen your commitment.

If you decide to skip this step, my honest expectation is that you will fail to achieve your goal. If you make it easy and safe to fail, you probably will.

At this point you may be wondering when we're going to get to the action steps. Where's the how-to part? Well, we're already into the action steps. *This is very much a part of the how-to.* We have to set things up so that you're very likely to take action. How are the other steps going to benefit you if you only read them but you don't actually do them? How many times have you read how-to info, said to yourself "I should do that," and then dropped the ball? We need to avoid that kind of outcome.

My intention is not to teach you the steps to generate passive income. That would be a waste of everyone's time, and it's already been done. My intention is that you actually *create* a new passive income stream for yourself. That's the end result I want you to achieve. I'm writing this for the people who are finally ready to begin receiving some passive income this year. I'm not writing for the ones who are just curious about it. If you're merely curious, that's fine, but please don't get in the way of us doers.

Are You In or Out?

This is the point where you must now decide: *Am I going to follow this as an active doer or not? Am I going to follow along with action and create a new stream of passive income, or am I going to sit on the sidelines and watch other people do it?*

If you aren't sure, then you're not a doer . . . at least not yet. Either get sure and commit to this, or this boat will sail without you. You may tell yourself that you can always come back to this later, but will you? I think it's fair to say that it's now or never.

You may wonder what this commitment will entail. Shouldn't you learn the action steps before you have to commit? Nope. That's not how it's done. You commit first, and then the steps appear. What more do you need? I'm personally coaching you through this whole thing. I've already done this multiple times, and countless others have done it as well. It's obviously a possible and achievable pursuit. And if you're really committed, then even if I drop the ball, you'll just continue on without me and learn what you need to learn elsewhere (just like I did).

Do you really have to commit in the dark? You're not actually committing in the dark, though. You're the one who's ultimately going to move this goal forward, not me. You're the light source here. I'm just the helper you've summoned into your reality to help you create this now.

What's the worst that will happen anyway? Even if you commit and fail, you're still going to learn some amazing things along the way. You'll see what you're made of. Worst case, you'll suffer some negative consequences, like a little embarrassment. Big deal. You'll live.

So are you in, or are you out? If you're not sure that you're in, you can be sure that you're out.

A year from now, what decision will you wish you made today?

Chapter 5

Jobs vs. Passive Income

Many people have the limiting belief that passive income is weird, unusual, complicated, or confusing. As I've mentioned previously, passive income isn't particularly difficult in practice. In many ways, earning a living through streams of passive income is easier than earning a living through a job or as an independent contractor, especially in the long run.

The difficult part has to do with getting comfortable with a passive income mindset.

To tackle this mindset issue, let's turn this around and look at it from the other side.

Suppose you were already very comfortable with passive income, just like I am. Imagine that you had many thousands of dollars coming in every month, more than enough to cover all your expenses. Whether you work or not, fresh income keeps flowing to you month after month and year after year, based on streams you set up years ago.

Imagine that this is your normal everyday reality. You've already been living like this for more than a decade.

Now imagine that a friend with a regular job tries to convince you that what you're doing is weird or unusual and that you should adopt his mindset, give up your passive income lifestyle, and get a regular job instead.

If a job-loving friend did this with me, here's what such a conversation might look like . . .

Friend: You know . . . you should join the world of real people and get a regular job. This passive income stuff you're doing is just too strange.

Me: It seems to work well enough. What's wrong with it?

Friend: Well . . . it's not what most people do. Most people get jobs.

Me: How does that work?

Friend: Basically you go to work for some other company, usually a corporation. You do the work, and they give you a paycheck.

Me: Okay. Is my paycheck somehow based on the value I contribute?

Friend: More or less.

Me: So will I receive a fair amount relative to my contribution?

Friend: Depends on what you mean by *fair.* Obviously they're not going to pay you 100% of what they think you're contributing. They have to make a profit as well.

Me: Well do I get 80% of it or something like that?

Friend: Realistically it's probably closer to 30% , but it's not tracked that precisely. They don't really know how much value you're contributing relative to everyone else. On larger teams it's especially difficult to know how much value any individual is contributing. So salaries invariably involve a lot of guesswork.

Me: Where does the rest of the value I create go?

Friend: It gets distributed in many different ways — as

income to investors and stockholders, to company profits, to corporate taxes, to higher pay for officers, to various perks like company picnics, and so on. That's for the higher-ups to decide, so it isn't really up to you.

Me: Do I at least get a share of those company profits?

Friend: Not usually, although some companies do have a profit-sharing plan, but even then they won't share all the profits . . . usually less than half. Sometimes you'll indirectly get a small cut, like in the form of a bonus.

Me: Hmmm . . . Do I have to work every day?

Friend: Usually just weekdays, but it depends on the job. You may also get a few weeks per year for vacation time.

Me: Only a few weeks? What if I want to travel for a month or two?

Friend: Well, you usually can't. Maybe if you save up vacation time for a few years, then they would let you, but it's not good to be gone so long at a stretch.

Me: Why does vacation time need to be saved up? Time passes on its own. If I can afford to go on vacation, why can't I just go?

Friend: Because they need you to work.

Me: What if I'm burned out and don't feel like working?

Friend: There's free coffee.

Me: Good coffee or bad coffee?

Friend: Depends on the job, but there's always a Starbucks nearby if they only serve Folgers in the office.

Me: Can I take my laptop to the Starbucks and work there?

Friend: Depends on the job, but usually not.

Me: Can I go on more vacations if I work from the road on my laptop now and then?

Friend: Not usually.

Me: Why not?

Friend: Well, they probably wouldn't trust you to work if you're out of the office too much.

Me: So they have to watch me work?

Friend: Basically, yes. But also some jobs are collaborative, so they want everyone together in the same place.

Me: I often do work now that's collaborative. We collaborate over the Internet or by phone.

Friend: Yup, some jobs are moving in that direction, but most employers still want you to show up each day.

Me: Where do I get to work?

Friend: That depends heavily on the type of job. For many office jobs, you'll work in a cubicle.

Me: What's a cubicle?

Friend: It's a subdivision in a larger room, delineated by short fuzzy walls. You should have enough room for a desk and a chair. Typically you'll have 50–80 square feet of space for yourself.

Me: So it's like the Shire?

Friend: Pretty much, but usually not as green.

Me: My home office is about 200 square feet, and it has its own bathroom and shower. But I can work wherever I want, so I'm not confined to that space.

Friend: Yeah, you won't get a space that size as a regular employee most likely, unless you work in management or some other high-value job that warrants its own office. That isn't what most employees get, but it isn't out of the question. It just depends on the job.

Me: Do I get to pick my own job title?

Friend: Usually it's assigned, but sometimes you can. It depends on the company.

Me: Can I pick *Master*?

Friend: Mmmm . . . probably not.

Me: What about the pay?

Friend: Well, you'd probably earn a lot less than you do now for doing the same kind of work. Just to give you an idea, the average salary for a blogger is about $17–38K per year.

Me: Wow . . . that's a lot less than I earn now passively, even when I'm on vacation. How would I even live on that?

Friend: Other people get by on that much. You'd have to cut back quite a bit, especially since you'll need more money for commuting (gas, car maintenance), professional work clothes if required, and various other expenses incurred by employees. But you might get a free company T-shirt and coffee mug and maybe a mouse pad if you're lucky, so it sort of balances out.

Me: Ouch. But what if I could somehow earn the same amount I do now, but from a job instead of from passive income?

Friend: That would be very unlikely, but if you did manage that, you'd pay a lot more in taxes, since this would all be W2 employee income. You can't use your business like you do now to lower your taxes.

Me: How much more in taxes are we talking?

Friend: The extra taxes you'd pay would be enough to buy a new car every year.

Me: That doesn't sound too appealing. Seems like it would be harder to get ahead if so much of each paycheck goes to taxes.

Friend: Yes, but the government understands this, so they make it look less painful by hiding a portion of those taxes, so it doesn't seem like your income is being taxed as heavily. You never receive that part of your salary in the first place. Some of your taxes are disguised in the form of taxes paid by your employer, like the employer's contribution to Social Security and Medicare for having you on the payroll. So even though your paycheck stub will report a certain base pay, your actual base pay (from your employer's and the government's perspective) is higher. You can bet that your employer is wanting to recoup those extra taxes from you in extra value you must contribute.

Me: I'm aware of this. U.S. tax laws are clearly hardest on regular W2 employees, who pay the highest taxes of anyone relative to their income. So why would people want to have their income allocated as W2?

Friend: Most people don't know any better. Besides, they wouldn't know what to do with all that extra money anyway. Lower pay keeps them out of trouble, and it ensures that they keep showing up for work. Gotta keep the economy going.

Me: All right.

Friend: There are some job perks too.

Me: Like what?

Friend: You get health insurance.

Me: I have that now, but I hardly ever use it since I prefer to just stay healthy.

Friend: Well, you could afford to be less healthy if you had a job, and you wouldn't have to pay for it.

Me: Hmmm . . .

Friend: Free coffee too.

Me: You said that already.

Friend: Did I mention that you can have as much as you want?

Me: Okay. So what kind of work would I do at a regular job?

Friend: That depends on the job, but big picture . . . it's usually something that supports the company's goals.

Me: Who sets these goals?

Friend: At a well-run company, the officers figure them out, with input from board members, key investors, and sometimes from employees too.

Me: Where can I see those goals?

Friend: Usually you don't get to, but sometimes they'll share snippets in the form of a company mission statement, a list of objectives, or perhaps a memo. But you're not really going to know what the company's true goals are. That's normally shared on a need-to-know basis only, and most employees don't need to know.

Me: Okay. So how do I know which goals to work on?

Friend: Usually your boss determines that, so you just do whatever your boss tells you.

Me: I have to have a boss?

Friend: Yup, everyone does. Even the CEO is accountable to the board and the shareholders.

Me: Okay, so what if my boss doesn't do a very good job of telling me what to do?

Friend: That often happens. You muddle through. Just make sure you look busy when you're being watched, and you should be ok. Personal accountability tends to be pretty low, so as long as you don't stand out as being obviously idle, you're probably safe.

Me: What if the boss and I disagree on how to achieve the company's goals?

Friend: That's where you start getting into company politics, which can be messy. Some people do what the boss says anyway, even when they know it won't work. Other people try to push back or negotiate. Sometimes that works, but sometimes they get marginalized or even let go if the boss doesn't like it. Usually people compromise somewhere in the middle.

Me: Are these compromises normally intelligent?

Friend: Not usually.

Me: If I do a good job of helping the company achieve its goals, do I get extra rewards for that?

Friend: Yes, sometimes. You might get a raise, a bonus, or a promotion. Or you might get intangible rewards like praise, appreciation, and recognition. Sometimes, however, you don't get anything more than your base pay.

Me: How do promotions work?

Friend: You get a new job title and have more responsibility, which usually comes with higher pay. Sometimes it means longer hours too.

Me: What if I come up with a really great idea, but it's not part of my assigned duties?

Friend: Ummm . . . yeah . . . don't do that.

Me: Why not?

Friend: You'll just be a rabble-rouser. The other employees won't like it if you try to upstage them, and they'll make your social life at work unpleasant till you back down.

Me: So if I try to work harder or smarter and get promoted faster, the other employees may try to hold me back?

Friend: Probably. Your boss may not like it very much either.

Me: My boss wouldn't like it? Why not? Isn't it part of his job to cultivate good talent?

Friend: Perhaps, but he wants to look good too. It's not good for him if one of his underlings is outshining him.

Me: That doesn't sound like an environment where I can really do my best work.

Friend: Yeah, but it's all good. Fortunately your best isn't required. You just need to get by. It's actually easier this way.

Me: But if I know I'm not doing my best, then won't I feel worse about myself? Won't that lower my self-esteem?

Friend: Sure, but you get used to it. Everyone adapts.

Me: So what is it like to work with a group where no one is doing their best, and everyone thinks less of themselves and their coworkers because of it?

Friend: Pretty boring actually. But again, you get used to it. The free coffee helps it go down easier.

Me: Okay, so let me get this straight. You're suggesting that I shut down all my passive income streams, go to work for someone else, get a boss and do what he says even if his decisions are unintelligent, do mediocre work instead of my best, socialize with people who also do mediocre work, work longer hours for less pay, take fewer and shorter vacations and ask permission to take them, and pay a great deal more in taxes?

Friend: Pretty much, yes. But you're overlooking the security aspect.

Me: What's secure about it?

Friend: Well, you'll get a steady paycheck.

Me: How steady? Does it ever end?

Friend: Well, sure it can end. You could get fired or laid off.

Me: Can I prevent myself from getting fired or laid off?

Friend: Not necessarily. It could happen due to circumstances beyond your control. Or you might just make a mistake. Or someone higher up may not like you.

Me: So how is that secure?

Friend: Well, it's mostly secure.

Me: So if I get fired or laid off, how much residual income will I continue to get?

Friend: Usually none. You might get a severance package for certain jobs, but that's only short-term for transitioning. For the most part, once your job ends, you stop getting paid.

Me: But currently I get paid whether I'm working or not. And I can't be fired or laid off.

Friend: Yeah, that's weird.

Me: Just feels normal to me.

Friend: Well, I know you're kind of set in your ways, but jobs are very popular. They obviously work for lots of people.

Me: What about finding a job? Does everyone get one automatically?

Friend: Oh, no. People have to seek them out and apply for them.

Me: How do they find jobs? Do they decide what they like doing and then find a job that lets them do it?

Friend: Usually it's not that simple. Most of the time they have to see what's available, and it probably won't match perfectly with what they really like.

Me: And once they find a job and select it, then they get hired?

Friend: No. Again, it's not that simple. It's a competitive marketplace. They have to apply, but they probably won't be chosen. They may have to apply to many jobs before they're offered one, and it may not be the one they most wanted. Also, millions of people who want jobs can't seem to get hired at all.

Me: This sounds very time consuming and stressful. What do they do if they can't find a job?

Friend: Well, they have to mooch off someone else to get by . . . off the government, off a relationship partner, off a friend or family member.

Me: And what if they still can't find a job, and no one lets them mooch anymore?

Friend: Then they might become homeless.

Me: That doesn't sound too secure to me.

Friend: Well, most people don't end up there. So it works okay overall. And being homeless isn't as bad as it seems. People cope.

Me: Do most people like their jobs?

Friend: No, at least 80% don't.

Me: So why do they keep going to work?

Friend: They need the money. And what choice do they have?

Me: They could earn money without a job.

Friend: Yeah, maybe . . . but who does that?

Me: I do.

Friend: Yeah, but you're weird.

Me: I appreciate your sharing all of this, but in a world that considers this job thing normal, I think I'll stick with my current approach, even if you think it's weird. I enjoy the work I do, I get paid well whether I work or not, I can travel whenever I want, I don't have a boss, I can't be fired or laid off, I don't feel I'm overpaying on taxes, and I can do my best without feeling pressured to be mediocre. Best of all, I get to use *Master* as my official title.

Friend: Sure, that all sounds good, but most people can't do it.

Me: Why not?

Friend: I don't think most people are smart enough.

Me: There are lots of not-so-bright people earning passive income. You'd be amazed at how much mental capacity is freed up when you don't have to deal with a boss or company politics . . . and when you don't hold yourself back doing mediocre work instead of your best . . . and when you aren't stressed about being potentially fired or laid off.

Friend: True, but those people are weird too.

Me: Perhaps.

Friend: Also, passive income is way too complicated for most people.

Me: If people can handle all the complexities of jobs, I think they'll find it a breeze to earn passive income. There's no job hunting, no resume, no application, no boss, no company politics, no need to save up vacation time, no risk of being fired, no commuting, and lower taxes. Yes, there's a different learning curve in the beginning, but if people can handle working for someone else, I think they can easily handle setting up passive income streams. And once they've done it once or twice, it's pretty straightforward after that.

Friend: Well, I'm still skeptical, so I suggest you give this some further thought. Again, jobs are very popular. I think you should give it a try.

Me: Do you think I'd like it?

Friend: No, but you'll get used to it. Trust me. It will all be fine. Again, it's very popular.

Me: Maybe for the free coffee.

Chapter 6

You Earn Passive Income by Being More Generous

Now that we've covered setting your passive income goal and a bit about the mindset of passive income — I hope you enjoyed the humor in the last chapter — let's explore the details of how to actually create passive income streams. We'll start out fairly high-level here and then drill down into the specifics in future posts.

Here are the 3 basic parts of an income generating method:

1. Value creation

2. Value delivery

3. Payment

Notice that these same 3 aspects can be applied to any basic income generation method. When you work at a regular job, for instance, you're probably going to create and deliver something of value to your employer, and then you receive payment for it.

So what's different about passive income? The difference stems mainly from the second aspect: how value is delivered.

When you generate active income such as with a regular job, your value delivery is usually done just *once*. Whatever work output you've created gets handed over to your employer.

The same goes for contract work. You do some work for a client (value creation), hand over that work (value delivery), and get paid.

With a passive income strategy, however, the idea is to deliver this value multiple times. Then you get paid multiple times, once for each delivery.

So the heart of a passive income strategy is found mainly in the approach to delivering value.

Passive Value Delivery

The words "passive income" suggest that it's the third aspect (payment) that defines the difference between passive and active income, but the main differences are usually found in the value delivery methods.

With an active income method, you hand over your work product once and get paid for it once. With a passive income method, your work product is delivered multiple times, and you get paid multiple times.

The *passive* element means that this value is being delivered without your direct personal effort. So you're using a method to get your work output into the hands of multiple customers, but you don't have to be the one personally delivering it. For example, when I publish a new article to my blog, it gets delivered to people all over the world automatically, but I don't have to personally send it to everyone. The value delivery is automated.

Why Just One Customer?

Now here's a good question to ask yourself: Why do you only have one customer?

A person with a job is just a business owner who sells to only one customer. If you take a passive income strategy and apply it to just one customer at a time, you have an active income strategy. One boss. One employer. One client at a time.

A person who generates passive income usually prefers to deliver value to multiple customers simultaneously. Another option is to repeatedly deliver value to the same customers over and over, but without having to create that value anew each time. A good example of this would be renting out property that you own. You can generate passive income this way even with a single customer since that customer can keep paying you rent every month.

When people shift from an active income to a passive income mindset, they usually start thinking about how to deliver value to more people. Instead of having just one customer for your work output, why not have 10 customers . . . or 100 . . . or 1,000? Why not have 1,000,000 customers?

How many people are you capable of helping?

Scaling Up

Note that with an active income strategy, income is a function of value creation. If you only have one employer, one client, or one customer for a particular work product, then in order to increase your income, you have to work harder, or you have to charge more for your creations.

But with a passive income strategy, you have an additional leverage point. You can deliver the same value more than once and get paid for each delivery. As it turns out, this is a powerful leverage point.

When you start thinking about how to scale your work, you'll often find that you could do the same core work but also serve more people than you do now. You'd simply need a different way to deliver your value.

For example, you could write software for one company and get a paycheck from them, but you could also develop and release your own software that lots of people can download and use.

You could work as an attorney and see one client at a time, or you could create and sell books with your best legal advice, thereby helping many more people.

Think about the work you do right now. How could you modify your work so that you can provide your value to many more people?

Chances are that your employer is already taking your active labor and applying a passive income strategy to it. You do the work one time, and they leverage it to generate long-term streams of income. Or you may be working to support the system your company developed to deliver passive income and capital gains to its investors and founders.

Sales are the lifeblood of any business. If you sell to only one customer, that isn't much blood, so you don't have much of a flow going there.

To enter the realm of passive income, start questioning the wisdom of running a business that sells to only one customer. And start thinking about how you could scale up the work you do, so you can deliver the value you're already capable of creating to more than one customer simultaneously.

Generally speaking, the way to create streams of passive income is to deliver your value to multiple customers simultaneously and to get paid multiple times. If you're going to work anyway, then you're already creating value for someone. Why sell to only one customer? Broaden your horizons, and realize that if one employer is willing to pay you for the value you're producing, chances are that someone else would be willing to pay you too — if only you weren't so clingy with your one and only customer.

Stop Being So Selfish With Your Value

I tend to regard people who use active income strategies as being more selfish and self-centered than those who use passive income strategies. That may sound harsh, but the truth is that active income earners aren't very good at sharing. They share their value with just one customer at a time, which in a world with billions of people is rather limiting, wouldn't you say?

People often refer to this as loyalty, but it's really just limited thinking. Besides, your employer may already be using this limited thinking against you as it generates passive income for others based on your active work output.

Passive income earners are constantly looking for ways to

put more value into the hands of more people. They want to be as generous as possible. They love to share. And so society rewards them with streams of passive income, so they get paid even when they aren't working.

Society doesn't care how hard you work. It doesn't care how creative you are. It only cares about the value you're actually getting into people's hands. That's what you get paid for — for value delivery — not for your ideas, or your long work days, or your intrinsic value as a human being.

We'll cover the details of how to do this later. For now, your homework is to start thinking about the value you're already delivering to people, and consider how you could scale it up to deliver this value to multiple people at the same time. It doesn't matter whether you have a job or not. What value do you deliver to your friends and family? Why do people bother spending time with you? What other forms of value could you provide if you made an effort? Hint: you don't actually have to be the one personally delivering this value. You just have to ensure that the delivery occurs.

Begin to step into the mindset of becoming a more generous provider of value to others. This is ultimately what passive income is all about.

Chapter 7

Is It Fair to Earn Passive Income?

Some people have asked whether it would be sustainable if everyone tried to earn passive income, so let's get that out of the way before we continue.

I think the supposition here is that certain jobs don't adapt well to passive income strategies, and therefore certain work is best suited to active income. Let's suppose that's true for the sake of argument.

Passive and active income strategies compete in the marketplace. People are free to choose either strategy. Most people choose active income. Why? I think the main reason is that they've been socially conditioned to choose this strategy. They probably make this choice without much knowledge of passive income strategies. Schooling, parents, and peers help train most people to choose active income.

Even if a lot more people started earning passive income and fewer people were willing to earn money as active income, I believe the market would adapt without skipping a beat. For critical tasks that could only be performed with ongoing labor, prices would rise, and therefore more people would be willing to perform those tasks.

Presently we have an oversupply of people who are looking for jobs, and we have a shortage of jobs for those people. So is it really wise to keep training more people to look for jobs? No, that would be foolish and will only make the problem worse. It will also cause salaries to drop, lowering people's standard of living.

I think a better solution is to teach passive income strategies and help some of those people make different choices. Passive income is a great choice in this economy since you won't need to find a job. In fact, you can actually help to stimulate more job creation.

Passive income has the effect of creating more jobs as well as supporting existing jobs. Whenever I create new passive income streams, I create income for other businesses. These generate revenue that helps cover the salaries of many employees.

Remember that passive income methods involve delivering value to more people than you probably could with an active income strategy. I see no reason to hold back on providing value. You may be providing different forms of value with a passive income strategy, but it's still a net gain for others if you increase your contribution.

If you license your book to a book publisher and receive passive income in the form of royalties on sales, the publisher may in turn pay people to perform specific jobs to keep their system running, and those employees may receive active income in the form of a salary. Your book deal helps to facilitate this and creates and sustains jobs for others.

Passive and active income strategies are mutually supportive. They are not opposites. I think it's healthy for both to co-exist.

I don't personally want a regular job, but I understand that

many people do, sometimes desperately so. I may poke fun at the regular job mindset now and then to get people to think about this more consciously and to consider alternatives, but I respect people's ability to make their own choices.

As for whether it's fair to earn passive income, I'd say it's more than fair. It's downright generous. As I've said previously, passive income tends to be more heavily rewarded (and less taxed) than active income. But passive income strategies can also add a lot of value to the economy, and so it makes sense to reward these strategies more heavily. By helping to create and sustain more jobs for others, you can actually generate significantly more tax revenue than you would if you earned the same amount via active income.

It's not uncommon for active income earners to think of passive income as a greedy strategy. The irony is that it's just as easy to regard active income earners as holding back and making a lesser contribution . . . contributing to just one employer when they could be serving many more people. The truth is that both strategies seek to contribute, just in different ways.

In the next several chapters, I'll cover some specific passive income strategies. I'll even demonstrate some of these strategies with specific examples from my own business, so you can better understand how they work.

Chapter 8

Passive Income Systems

To generate passive income, you need a way to maintain your income without having to do so much grunt work to keep it going. If you have to keep working each day to avoid seeing your income drop, then you're earning active income, not passive income. Passive income continues to flow even when you aren't actively working.

Many forms of passive income still require daily or weekly maintenance activities, such as fulfilling orders or handling customer service, but this doesn't mean that you have to perform those maintenance tasks yourself. You may delegate such tasks to other people, to businesses, or to technology. For your income to be passive (meaning that you don't have to do much to maintain your cashflow), you need to remove items from your plate, but those items still need to get done.

A *passive income system* is a form of delegation. What is being delegated, and to whom? How will the necessary active tasks be handled if you won't be doing them yourself? Your passive income system must provide these answers.

I love delegating to technology because it's fast, efficient, consistent, and inexpensive. Technology also tends to scale well, meaning that you can add more computing resources, which generally requires little more than paying for those resources. This works well for an Internet business.

For example, I delegate the distribution of my blog posts to my web server. I post them to my server when I click the "Publish" button, and then various hardware and software does the rest. Without this technology I would have to use some other distribution method. Technology is so ubiquitous these days that it's easy to overlook what it does for us and take it for granted, but it can perform a vital role in any passive income system. Without this technology, what would it take to distribute copies of every article I've written to millions of monthly readers around the globe every month? It would be a massive effort if this had to be performed by human hands.

Notice then that when you rely on technology to communicate, you're already taking advantage of passive systems. Your messages pass through equipment that's designed, built, and maintained by others. You may not be paying those people directly, but they're working for you every day. You're already taking advantage of these systems now. So if you currently rely on such systems for your communication needs, then why not leverage them to handle your income as well?

You can also delegate tasks to other people and to businesses to get them off your plate. In a typical affiliate deal, you may delegate the order processing, fulfillment, and customer service to another company. For example, if you use Amazon's affiliate program to sell items, you're effectively delegating a significant portion of the work to Amazon. From your perspective, an affiliate sale may seem very passive, but that's because Amazon provides the active labor to make your affiliate commissions possible.

Build or Borrow

To employ your own passive income system, you have several options:

1. You can design and build your own passive income system from scratch.

2. You can learn how other people earn passive income and try to copy their approach.

3. You can use someone else's system as-is (usually by paying for the privilege).

4. You can do a combination of any of the above.

I've used all of these approaches at different times. I can't offer a general recommendation for one of these above the others though. The most intelligent choice depends on a variety of factors including time constraints, budget constraints, personal strengths, and personal goals.

If you're up for a real challenge, it can be very rewarding to design and implement your own passive income system from scratch. The upside to this approach is that you invented it, so you know its inner workings, and you can customize it all you want. The downside is that this method can take a lot of work, and it may be quite a while before the first income streams start flowing. Innovation is risky. Sometimes the risk pays off. Sometimes it doesn't.

More commonly, people borrow ideas from each other. Why reinvent the wheel? Learn what works for other people, and use similar methods for yourself. There are plenty of books and systems authored by entrepreneurs who are happy to teach you how to do what they did. Some people are willing to share details of their systems for free, while others only share this info for a fee. Even when there is a fee, buying someone else's system can save you a tremendous amount of time and energy.

When I was trying to build some sales for my computer games during the 1990s, I bought a book called *How to Sell Your Software* by Bob Schenot. Bob shared the details of his system, and I was able to adapt much of his advice to my own business, which saved me a lot of time. That system would seem very dated today (it was largely pre-Internet), but it got me off to a good start in building my own direct sales system.

A seemingly inexpensive approach is to use someone else's system as-is. An example of this is licensing your book to a book publisher or selling your book via Amazon. This may seem like a good deal since you don't have to pay anything up front, but it can be a lot more expensive if you do well because you may have to give away a significant percentage of your sales to the system provider. This approach tends to be the easiest for getting started. System providers in this category may be very good at processing orders and handling customer service, but they usually don't provide much marketing assistance, so it may be hard for you to get noticed with them. That said, they can do an awful lot of work for you, making your income streams very passive.

The good news is that you don't have to understand how to build a passive income system from scratch in order to use one, just as you don't need to know how to build a computer from scratch in order to use it.

My personal favorite is the hybrid approach. I pick up many good ideas from others, but I like to put my own spin on things and keep tweaking my passive income streams as I go. I rarely use other people's systems as-is, often because I find their marketing methods a mismatch for my audience, so at the very least, I still need to tweak the marketing elements even if the underlying product or service is a good fit.

To Buy or Not to Buy

One question that will surely come up for you is whether or not you should buy into someone else's system, such as by paying for their knowledge or resources.

Generally I do think this is a good idea, especially when you're first starting out, but only if you're cautious about it. You can waste a lot of money buying low-quality money-making systems from random Internet marketers. On the other hand, paying for a good system can also deliver tremendous value. You can learn in a short period of time what took someone else years or even decades of painstaking work to piece together.

I used to be a bit over-eager in paying for what seemed like premium knowledge in this area, and I wasted money on what turned out to be fluffy or outdated info. Then I cut back massively and became very stingy, which caused me to miss some easy opportunities. And finally I settled into what I feel is a more practical and realistic attitude. I'm willing to pay for systems know-how if I think I'll be able to apply it effectively and if the info comes from a quality source. For me a quality source is someone who seems to genuinely want to help people understand and apply the methods they teach, rather than just selling low-quality info to make more money. Also, a quality system is one that's already been proven to work under real-world conditions.

Usually when I pay for systems knowledge these days, I'm not looking to implement someone else's system as-is. I'm simply looking for a few fresh ideas I can use to upgrade my existing systems. What are the latest and greatest ideas I might otherwise miss?

I know that when it comes to marketing, the people who sell these systems may try to push my emotional buttons and offer extra incentives to get me to buy. I do my best to ignore those sales tactics and look at the potential value more objectively.

Since I know people want to know this, I'll share a couple of specific recommendations for systems you can use to generate passive income streams online today.

Site Build-It

I've been recommending Site Build-It (SBI) since early 2008, referring thousands of new customers to them. I still wholeheartedly recommend this service today for its outstanding mix of technology, tools, hosting, and education. They sought to be an all-in-one solution that helps people build successful online businesses (not just websites), and they really deliver on that.

SBI continues to update its technology, and they had a major update not long ago, so now it's even more robust and modern than it was when I first began recommending it.

SBI also hosts an active discussion forum where its members share tips and strategies on a daily basis. That alone is a treasure trove of useful information . . . not to mention an ongoing support resource for SBI members.

SBI charges a very reasonable subscription fee for its service. The annual cost for an SBI site is less than what I pay for a single month of web hosting for StevePavlina.com. SBI sites are certainly capable of generating at least as much passive income as I do, and many SBIers own multiple sites. This is a very cost effective solution if you're interested in generating passive income with a website that you own.

I recommend SBI especially if you have a topic you're very interested in, or you have some knowledge you'd like to share. Instead of constantly sharing ideas on your Facebook page, you could be sharing them on your own website and using that to generate traffic. Then you can monetize that traffic in various ways to generate income.

I recommend SBI because people are making real money with it, they provide a solid all-in-one solution, and it's very inexpensive relative to the value they provide.

For details on SBI, see my review here:

https://stevepavlina.com/site-build-it/

Get Rich With Ebooks

My book publisher Hay House informed me yesterday that ebook sales are expected to nearly double this year. We're in a unique time where the demand for ebooks is growing so much faster than the supply, partly because tablet computers have been selling like crazy. There's a hungry demand for ebooks that can be read on these devices.

I spent the past week in Canada, and during my flights I did some ebook reading on my iPhone. Despite the small screen, I found it very pleasant to use for reading, and I know I'm not alone. The people in the aisle across from me on one flight were reading ebooks on their iPads. This trend towards ebook mobility is only going to continue.

Last night I was discussing the inevitable contraction of print book publishing with my friend Stewart Emery. Stewart co-authored *Success Built to Last,* and he's an influential figure in the book publishing industry. A while back he predicted that either Borders or Barnes & Noble would be out of business within two years. Two years later (almost exactly) Borders went bankrupt, and Barnes & Noble was saved by shifting their focus to ebooks with the Nook.

For my own book, I can also see that sales of the Kindle version are exceeding sales of the paperback and hardcover versions combined. I expect this gap to widen even more over the next five years.

This situation creates some unusual opportunities for ebook authors. Eventually the supply will catch up, but for now the demand is increasing at a much faster rate. There are still far more print books than ebooks on the market, but the sales momentum is all on the ebook side. This is creating something of a gold rush for ebook authors.

Vic Johnson noticed this trend, and he jumped on it. To date he's earned more than $7 million from ebooks. He offers a very thorough course on how to do what he does, appropriately named *Getting Rich With Ebooks:*

http://www.vicjohnson.com/getrichebooks.htm

I've gone through this course myself and learned quite a lot from it. I also spoke to Vic directly. He was broke, and selling ebooks became his ticket to wealth, which explains why he's so passionate about them. I recommend checking out Vic's course and his system for creating and selling ebooks. This unusual demand-supply situation won't last forever.

This trend is similar to the advantage I capitalized on when

I started my blog in 2004; back then the demand was growing so much faster than the supply, and many people who started blogs around the same time I did saw significant traffic growth as public interest in blogs grew and grew. If you're just starting a blog today, however, you're pretty late to the game since now the field is much more crowded.

The interesting twist here is that Vic doesn't even write most of the content he sells. He's earned quite a lot of money from repackaging public-domain works and from using ghostwriters to create content for him. He explains how to do this in his program, including how to identify opportunities for new ebooks you can sell.

Take note that if you use Vic's system, you can even use any of the articles or podcasts on my website to create your own ebooks since they're all uncopyrighted. If you search on my name at Amazon.com, you'll see that dozens of ebooks based on my content have already been released by others.

I can see that people are making a lot of amateurish mistakes in trying to repackage and resell my content, however, and that's going to hurt their sales. They'd likely be doing much better if they went through Vic's program first since he shares many optimization tips to increase sales. It's fine with me if people want to turn my content into ebooks to sell, but I'd love to see them do even better since it means the ideas will spread further.

Vic's system is a good choice if your writing skills aren't so great or if you have doubts about your ability to create high quality content on your own. If, on the other hand, you love to write like I do, then you can also use Vic's program to help you research, market, and sell your own ebooks effectively.

I think it's well worth the money, and Vic sells it with a try-before-you-buy model that makes it easy to get started.

I've already written a book (published by Hay House), so I've been through the whole publishing process and know what it's like. Nevertheless I still picked up some golden nuggets from Vic's program that I wasn't previously aware of. I also got a kick of out his enthusiasm, and I liked his down-to-earth style.

I think Vic's program will appeal to a lot of people who want passive income since it does not require that you have a website, nor does it require that you create one. Vic teaches you how to earn income using other websites to sell your ebook for you. You can still create a website to help sell your ebook, but that part is optional.

I like that Vic is very generous with his content, so he includes tons of extra bonuses and resources to help you with the practical details. He even tells you which specific service providers he uses and gives you their contact info.

Vic's program and SBI can complement each other quite nicely, so this isn't an either-or situation. You could easily create an SBI site and an ebook on the same topic. Your SBI site can help sell your ebook, and your ebook can help promote your SBI site. I enjoy this type of relationships between my book and my website, for instance — they both help to promote each other.

I used a similar combo strategy when I ran my computer games business. I sold the games through my own website, but I also posted my game demos to hundreds of software and game download sites. The download sites helped drive traffic to my website, where people could buy the full versions of my games. Vic uses a similar strategy, using inexpensive ebooks to drive traffic to his websites. He makes good money from the ebooks, and he also makes money from his websites, which can sell other products and services in addition to ebooks.

Passive Income From Real Estate

Real estate investing is one of the most common ways that people become wealthy.

You can buy real estate such as houses, apartment buildings, office space, retail space, etc. and rent it out. You can also make money from the appreciation, assuming that real estate prices rise while you own the property.

When renting a property, it's nice if you can create a positive cashflow, meaning that your monthly rents provide enough to cover your mortgages, upkeep, property taxes, and other expenses and still leave you with some profit. Note that as you pay down the mortgages (which is essentially being done by your tenants), you will gradually own more equity in the property. You can then borrow against this equity to fund more investments, or you can sell it and cash out.

Real estate investment has some tax advantages too. One role of government is to help ensure access to housing for its citizens, and so tax laws encourage real estate development and investing.

While real estate investing can be done in ways that require a lot of cash, with some creativity you can do deals that don't require tying up a lot of money — and still generate passive income for yourself. In this capacity you can also act as a real estate dealmaker, putting deals together that other people will execute. For instance, you could assemble a proposal for a new shopping center, help get key tenants interested, and then sell the deal to a real estate developer in exchange for a cut of the revenue. This is way beyond my current expertise, but I've heard of people making good money doing these kinds of deals.

Many businesses and organizations hold a great deal of wealth in the form of real estate. For example, McDonald's not only makes money from selling dead cows; they also own many valuable street corners around the world. The Catholic Church is also a major land owner.

As your investments increase in value and your equity increases, you can borrow against your equity to buy more property, thereby increasing your holdings over time. Of course there's a risk of overextending yourself. Many real estate investors have gone bust when their over-leveraged investments sank in value, and they ended up owing more than their properties were worth while also dealing with tenants who could no longer pay the rent.

I can't share much about real estate investing since I've never been into it. I've read several books on the subject out of curiosity, but providing housing and office/retail space to tenants just doesn't excite me. I think this would be a decent way to generate passive income for someone who is patient, can be disciplined enough to stick to a long-term plan, and who knows a lot about property and is good at assessing what a property is worth.

If this type of investment interests you, please don't let my personal preferences dissuade you from investigating it fully. Libraries have plenty of books on how to invest profitably in real estate, and I'm sure there are plenty of websites and forums where you can find good advice from experienced investors.

Even though it's not my cup of tea, I wanted to mention real estate investing as part of the passive income material since it's a common path that people use to generate passive income and long-term wealth.

Your Passive Income System Preferences

My goal in this article is to get you thinking about what kind of system you'd like to use to generate your own passive income streams. Do you want an income-generating website? Are you leaning towards having a product to sell on other people's websites? Would you like a system that incorporates both? Or do you want to do something wildly different?

Think about your strengths. A good system will allow you to leverage your strengths while delegating the areas where you're weakest. Are you a content machine like me where you need a system to provide an effective publishing platform and a way to monetize your work? Would you feel more comfortable selling someone else's product or service? Does selling turn you off, and would you prefer to delegate the selling aspect as well?

When it comes to passive income systems, the key test is whether your system works in the real world. You can dream up whatever you like, but dreams aren't streams.

A good passive income system generate results. If you've never created your own system from scratch, I recommend borrowing someone else's system if you want to reach your goal quickly. Otherwise if you prefer a bigger challenge and don't mind investing a lot more of your time and energy up front, you're always free to roll your own.

Once you've had the experience of working with someone else's system, you may decide to keep using it, you may experiment with different systems, or you may tackle the challenge of rolling your own system. There's no right or wrong way to do it.

But I'd suggest that for your first stream of passive income, it's much easier to simply borrow and apply someone else's system, even if you have to pay for it. A good system looks simple, but that's because it hides so many implementation details. For passive income, this is a good thing. Handling too many details yourself throws you back into the realm of active income.

A good passive income system will normally employ many different income-generating strategies simultaneously, weaving them into a congruent tapestry. This is similar to how a computer integrates many different hardware and software components that function well as a unit.

We can also learn a lot by breaking out and studying the individual components of a passive income system, and that's what I'll be sharing next. While I still recommend borrowing someone else's system to get started, learning the details of how the different elements work together is still very helpful since you'll probably want to tweak and extend what you learn from others.

Loving Your System

At this point you don't have to commit to a particular passive income system approach just yet. You'll eventually need to make such a commitment, but for now I just want you to familiarize yourself with some options and start giving this some thought.

It's important to cultivate a healthy relationship with the passive income system you'll use. If you love your system, you'll use it. If you don't like it so much, you'll procrastinate.

I don't do real estate investing to generate passive income because it would bore me to tears, and I wouldn't feel like

I'm contributing much. Some people may be very passionate about real-estate investing, but it's a bad fit for my personality and values.

On the other hand, I love blogging. I love that when I have an idea, I can get it out of my head and share it with thousands of people that same day. I love that my work is permanently archived and accessible 24/7 to anyone with an Internet connection. I'm not very patient, so when I have an inspired idea, I like to share it immediately. I love the passive income system that supports my blogging because it allows me to provide a tremendous amount of value for free without feeling I have to hold back or to charge money for every little thing. I like sharing, and the system I use allows me to do that abundantly.

I don't want you to make the mistake of adopting a passive income system that you merely tolerate. I want you to have a system that you truly appreciate. Offload the work that you don't enjoy, so you can do more of what you love. When you do what you love, you'll contribute more, and that's better for everyone.

Chapter 9

How to Earn Passive Income from Intellectual Property

In this chapter, we'll explore a number of strategies for earning passive income. Let's begin with one of my personal favorites.

Intellectual Property

Intellectual property refers to mental creations that are associated with legally recognized rights, such as material that can be copyrighted, trademarked, or patented. This includes articles, books, music, movies, artwork, photographs, comics, software, logos, and more.

Mere ideas do not generally qualify as intellectual property. It's the expression of the idea that's legally protected. You cannot claim the idea of poetry as your intellectual property, but you can copyright an original poem you've written, which gives you certain exclusive rights to that poem.

Since intellectual property is generally easy and inexpensive to duplicate, especially when it's in digital form, it's a great candidate for creating streams of passive income. You can deliver value to people simply by copying and sharing some data, and this process can be automated or outsourced.

To create a piece of intellectual property may involve a good deal of work, but that work need only be done once. After that, the property can be duplicated and shared with many people. You could potentially still be generating earnings 50 years from now for a piece of intellectual property you create today.

For instance, you can write a book once and then generate income from direct sales of the book or royalties from a book publisher. You can also earn income by selling the associated movie and merchandising rights.

Self-Publishing

Once you create a piece of intellectual property, one option is to sell it yourself and see if people will buy it from you.

This works well if you have a following or can build one. For people who are just starting out, it's going to take a while to build that following, usually years. If you're patient and persistent, this approach can really pay off though.

I used this approach with my games business. It took time to build a following, but I eventually got there. The only real way to fail is to give up, which is of course what most people do.

One of the leverage points for self-publishing is lead generation. This means finding a way to attract people who might be interested in your product. One way to do this is with advertising, but that can be risky and costly, so I don't recommend it for most people.

My favorite method of lead generation is to give away a lot of quality free content. With my games business, I offered free game demos and submitted them to hundreds of game and software downloads.

Note that putting up free content on a website with no traffic is not lead generation. Nobody will see it. You have to get your free stuff into people's hands, meaning that you have to put it where there's traffic. If you don't have the traffic, then put your free content somewhere other than your own website. The free content can then refer people back to your website, where they can buy something from you directly.

When you generate leads, don't let them fizzle out. Try to collect them. People often need to be exposed to an offer multiple times before they're willing to buy anything, so if someone visits your website but doesn't buy right away, give them other options to stay in your communication loop, such as by subscribing to your blog or newsletter or by following you on Twitter or Facebook.

As you generate leads over time, some of them will subscribe to one of your lists, so you can still communicate with them.

For my newsletter I use the service Aweber:

https://www.aweber.com/

I like this service and find it reliable, and the interface isn't overly complicated. In a typical issue I provide a new article (that doesn't appear on my blog — this is to reward subscribers), and there's usually at least one promotional offer in my newsletter that can help generate income. Worst case, I may just include a link soliciting donations.

Some people really push hard on the newsletters, sending them almost daily. I typically send mine about once a month, but I'm not perfectly regular about it. I've sent out 4 issues so far this year. If you wish to subscribe to see what it looks like — or to see what you're missing — you can sign up here:

https://stevepavlina.com/newsletter/

Of course I don't spam people or sell their email addresses, so all you get is the newsletter, and you can easily unsubscribe by clicking a link at the bottom of any issue.

To process sales you may need a merchant account and a shopping cart. It's been years since I shopped for a merchant account, so I don't know what kind of deals are available today. Try Googling "merchant account" to see if you can find a decent recommendation or review site for merchant accounts. You can also process orders via PayPal if you wish; they can handle credit card orders from non-PayPal customers, and their rates are competitive.

Self-publishing is a long road. It's definitely not a good choice for ADHD types. This is for the builders who enjoy creating something to endure.

The main advantage to self-publishing is that once you have it figured out, you're pretty much golden. As you learn what works for you and what doesn't, you can line up a string of repeat successes.

Licensing

Even though we speak of *selling* intellectual property products like ebooks and videos, what we're really doing is licensing them. The information within isn't actually being sold since no transfer of rights occurs. What's being sold is a license to use that information, and often the license is limited to a specific purpose. You might also sell the physical media that stores the information, like a CD or DVD.

Licensing is more obvious with software which often includes a license agreement. You may have to agree to its terms in order to use the software.

In a broader sense, you can license your intellectual property to other entities, who can then exploit it to generate revenue, and depending on how you structure the deal, you can earn a cut of that revenue stream. This is what happens when you sign a publishing deal with a book publisher. They sell the book, and you receive royalties from the sales.

Some companies make millions from licensing their intellectual property for various uses. Look at the thousands of products with Disney characters on them, for instance. Disney earns a bundle in licensing fees for those products. Could you create the next Mickey Mouse?

Here are some more examples of what you can do with intellectual property:

Design a T-shirt, and license your design to a T-shirt company in exchange for a small cut of the sales

Take some scenic photographs, and license them to a postcard publisher

Record some relaxing music, and license it to people who sell meditation audio programs

Write a new iPad or iPhone app, and sell it through iTunes

Write an ebook, and sell it through Amazon.com

Invent a cartoon character, and license it to a toy company to create stuffed animals

My ex-mother-in-law is an artist, and many years ago she licensed the artwork from some of her paintings to a greeting-card company. She earned royalties from the sales of those greeting cards.

Don't let the word *licensing* scare you. Licensing simply means "giving permission." Normally when you license work you created, you and the other party will sign a contract to spell out the terms. You can have a lawyer draft one for you, find boilerplate agreements online, or create your own.

Licensing Agreements

I paid lawyers to draft my first few licensing agreements, and once I became familiar with the key terms, I could easily write my own agreements, using what the lawyers created as a reference. Depending on the complexity of the agreement, it would cost me anywhere from several hundred dollars to a few thousand dollars to have a lawyer draft it for me. I would only do this if the deal was likely to generate more than enough income to cover the legal fees.

If I have a complicated licensing deal to negotiate, or if there are contract terms I'm not familiar with, then I'll consult with a lawyer to handle the tricky bits. I used a lawyer to help out with my book deal in 2007, which cost me $2,000. She helped me negotiate for better terms in some parts of the agreement, which I feel more than made up for the cost of her services.

Legal bills can add up quickly, but for deals where a lot of money is involved, the professional help can be well worth the expense.

Often you don't have to draft a licensing agreement yourself since they other party may provide one. Publishers do this as a matter of course. Then you only have to review it and suggest changes. I've rarely signed a licensing agreement without asking for something to be changed.

If you're broke or want to learn how to draft licensing agreements on your own, a good source for info is Nolo Press:

https://www.nolo.com/

They sell many quality books, software, and do-it-yourself legal kits.

Re-Licensing

If you create some intellectual property that can be licensed, you can even grant someone else the right to license your creation for you, usually by giving them a share of the revenue streams. For instance, my book *Personal Development for Smart People* was recently published in Polish. I didn't handle that deal; my publisher Hay House did. I didn't even know about it until I received two copies of the Polish edition in the mail. Hay House isn't publishing the book in Polish though. Hay House relicensed my book to a Polish publisher, which paid Hay House for those rights, and then Hay House and I split that money in accordance with our agreement. I gave Hay House the right to relicense my book to other publishers around the globe.

What do you do if you're a creative type who can create interesting intellectual property, but you aren't any good at selling or licensing it? Team up with someone who can handle the selling and licensing for you.

If I had retained the global licensing rights for my book, I could have done those foreign deals myself and kept all the money. But would I have done that as well as Hay House has been doing? Maybe . . . maybe not. They have connections and foreign rights managers and knowledge of different markets to put those deals together. That's why my book is in so many different languages now. If I tried to do it myself, I might have gotten some results, but it would have been much more time consuming and expensive to do it on my own, and I'm not giving up so much money to have Hay House handle this anyway.

Agents

When I ran my computer games business during the 90s, I knew how to create a game, but I didn't know how to get them published. My first method was to go to CompUSA, look at a bunch of game boxes, and get the addresses of as many publishers as I could. Then I snail-mailed a letter of introduction to dozens of them. Maybe 3 or 4 wrote or called back. None of those inquires resulted in deals, however. This was a rather naive shotgun approach but not very well targeted. I even got at least one in-person meeting this way, but it was clear the publisher wasn't a good match for the kinds of games I wanted to write.

Eventually I got introduced to a game agency by some other contact. Game agents act as brokers between game developers and game publishers, helping to create deals. I met with them and liked the idea of working with them. They helped me figure out what kinds of games to develop based on market trends, they set up meetings with publishers and helped me try to secure and negotiate deals. If they could get me a deal, they would get a percentage of whatever revenue I received, so it was no money out of pocket for me.

Usually I met publishers at conferences like E3 or the Game

Developers Conference, but sometimes I flew to their offices. My agent set up these meetings. Fortunately E3 was in L.A. where I lived, except for a few stupid years when they moved it to Atlanta, so that was convenient. I remember some sleepless nights preparing last-minute demo updates for these conferences.

For me, this approach was hit and miss. I landed some deals this way, but they weren't good deals. Some money came in ($120K in advances), but no games ever got published and released. I can't fully blame the agent for this. Suffice it to say there are a some truly bad apples in game publishing. The recent conflict between Activision and the Call of Duty developers reminds me of the kind of crap I had to deal with back then.

Be Cautious

That said, I later did some nicely lucrative game licensing deals, but I learned to be very selective about which publishers I worked with. When it comes to licensing, it can be more important to avoid bad deals than it is to land good ones. If you're going to get into this form of income generation, it can really pay off, but you may be risking a bloody nose now and then.

My best advice for evaluating a potential licensing partner is to do your homework. Get in touch with people who've worked with that potential partner, and ask if they're willing to share their experiences. Listen to what they say, and take it to heart.

I once did this when a game publisher approached me for a licensing deal. Their website had a list of developers they'd worked with in the past. I emailed all those developers (about

6 of them), and they all wrote back. Without exception what they told me was very specific and very negative. None of those developers had seen a dime in royalties. This publisher was ripping them off, selling their games in other countries and paying them nothing. Needless to say, I never worked with them, and I shared what I learned with other developers I knew to make sure they avoided this trap.

Dealmaking

Once you get good at licensing, you can generate new revenue streams by acting as a dealmaker. This may seem daunting if you've never done it before, but with practice it can be a lot of fun. You can get paid to act as a matchmaker.

Many years ago I licensed a computer game from a small game developer, including the right to re-license it. I published and sold the game through my own company, but I also turned around and re-licensed it to another publisher. This generated an extra stream of royalties, which I split with the developer as we had previously agreed. Could the developer have done this deal on his own? Maybe . . . but it would have taken him a lot longer. It was easy for me to close this deal quickly because I already had the connection with the right publisher.

Notice in this case that I didn't create or own the game, and I didn't own the other publisher's business or sales outlets. I just put the deal together, which generated income for the publisher and the developer — and for me as well. So please note that you can create streams of passive income from intellectual property even if you don't own the property or the sales platform. You can get a cut of the action for being the dealmaker, and deservedly so.

For several years I've worked with a guy who helps me find good joint venture deals. He's well connected in the personal development field and seems to spend most of his working time on the phone. He knows people who have great products and services. And he knows people who have sizable audiences like me. He connects one with the other, helps massage the deals into place, and enjoys a share of the revenue created by these deals. These income streams have paid off his mortgage. He didn't receive any special training for this, but through life experience he discovered that he was good at introducing people to each other, and he found a great way to turn that into multiple streams of income. On top of that, he recorded and produced his own music album, and he'll begin selling that soon as well. The deals I've done with him thus far have generated revenue for me well into the six figure range. Note that he gets paid not for the introductions (i.e. , not a finder's fee); he gets paid a small percentage of revenue from each deal he helps to close.

If someone brought you an easy-to-close deal that earned you an extra $1,000 per month, would you be willing to pay them $100 per month from that revenue stream for doing the legwork?

Some people are so good at dealmaking that they can generate millions in passive income with just a few phone calls. There's real value in connecting two or more people or businesses that can synergize their resources, if only they knew of each other's existence.

Creativity

Intellectual property is a nice choice for creative people because it's so flexible. You can create a piece of property once and then license/sell it in many different forms.

I also love that you don't need a lot of money to create intellectual property. I wrote my best selling computer game when I was dead broke. Its budget was basically $0. It didn't cost me anything to write my book either. You can create a great deal of content for free.

However, because the barrier to entry is so low, it means that lots of people are going to attempt this. The vast majority won't be any good, but this does create a crowding effect. Even if you're good at what you do, it may take some time to separate yourself from the mosh pit of wannabes, especially in the eyes of people you'd like to work with.

When you create something, try not to wrap your self-esteem around it. In the beginning you're probably going to suck. That's okay. Everyone but Mozart sucks initially. Keep practicing and honing your skills, and you'll get better.

I love doing creative work, so I've created a great deal of intellectual property, including software, several computer games, game characters, a book, articles, podcasts, newsletters, logos, speeches, workshops, poetry, signs, music, artwork, and more.

Being creative isn't enough if you want to turn your creations into income streams. Selling, licensing, and dealmaking are important skills as well, and I suggest that you try to respect these roles as much as you respect the content creation side. If you're unwilling to develop those related skill sets, then give some serious thought to partnering up with someone who can perform those roles. If you can convince them of your creative genius, it's a great opportunity for them as well. It certainly worked out well for Steve Jobs acting as dealmaker for Steve Wozniak in the early days of Apple Computer.

Chapter 10

Passive Income is Not an Escape

If your motivation for passive income is escape, you'll most likely fail. Passive income is fuel to expand what you're already doing. Trying to add fuel to what you don't want is a recipe for self-sabotage. You will give up before you get very far.

Trying to build passive income streams on top of a lifestyle you dislike is like doing weight training with incorrect form and then trying to add more weight. You're only going to hurt yourself if you proceed. It's not an intelligent approach.

If you don't like your lifestyle, it's important to fix that first. Don't think you can escape it by creating streams of passive income. It won't work.

My advice would be to first transition to active income sources where you can do work you enjoy. Then you can build upon that with passive income to serve even more people and extend the value you're able to provide.

So if you work as a health coach and mostly enjoy that kind of work, you can expand your service with something like an online course or an ebook or a website, which will allow you to passively provide value to people even when you're not available to help them one on one. This in turn will allow you to earn passive income. Passive income is a side effect of providing passive value.

But if you hate your current work and try to escape it with passive income, your work will be a constant albatross around your neck that drags you down. The real problem is your low standards and low self-esteem. Why are you currently willing to do work you dislike in exchange for money? Don't you deserve any better than this? This mindset is a bankrupt one. It means you'll never deliver your best service, and so your income will be depressed as well.

If you try to generate passive income from this place, I can tell you what will happen. Your willingness to do work you don't enjoy in exchange for money will carry over and infect your approach to passive income. Your focus will be on the money. You'll be thinking that if you can earn enough passive income, you can finally quit doing work you don't enjoy. So you'll pick something that you think will make money, and it will also require doing work you don't particularly enjoy — because that's where your mind is. You may try to make a website, even though you don't like making and running websites. Or you may try blogging even though you don't like writing. Or you'll try to write your own ebook even though you don't care to become an author. But your heart won't be in the work, so you'll burn out within a matter of months. You'll quit.

This is nothing but a repeat of the same failed strategy you've used on the active income side, except that with active income you may have a boss, coworkers, and enough bills to ensure that you keep showing up. Passive income is usually much easier to quit.

It's your unwillingness to demand enjoyment and fulfillment from your work that's the real issue you must deal with first.

Passive income won't cure your willingness to sacrifice your happiness for pay. If your mindset is infected by the idea of doing work you dislike in exchange for pay, then you are living with incorrect form. If you try to carry this incorrect form over to the passive income side, you will fail. You won't enjoy the work enough or see the point of it. You will quit.

So before you get all gung ho about setting up passive income streams, pause for a moment and check your form first. Are you living with correct form right now? Do you require fulfillment and happiness from your day job? Are you doing your best work? Do you feel motivated to work each day because you get to do what you enjoy?

Sure you may have some tedious tasks now and then, but what's the big picture? Overall, would you say that you like the way you're currently living and wish to expand it further? If so, then you're a good candidate for passive income. If not, then you need to stop and fix your form first.

Again, if you're willing to do work you dislike in exchange for pay, you're going to take that same wonky mindset with you as you pursue passive income. But this mindset isn't effective. It causes you to hold back, wallow in low standards, do work you feel is undignified, and give much less than your best effort. That isn't good enough for effective weight training, and it isn't good enough for generating passive income either . . . unless you only desire a mere trickle of results.

Fix your form first if it needs fixing. Make happiness a true priority in your life now — before you try to extend it with passive income. Otherwise you will be just as miserable on the passive side as you would on the active side, and who's going to work for something like that? You'll surely sabotage your results before you get very far at all.

Passive income is expansion, not escape. Creating passive income streams will add fuel to your current lifestyle, helping to extend and expand it. If you don't want to extend and expand what you already have, then make those adjustments while you still can. Don't try to build something that would make you feel even worse.

Chapter 11

Are You Still Broadcasting Doubt?

As you read through this passive income series, suppose you start seriously thinking about creating your own passive income streams. You talk about some ideas with your friends and family, and you get a negative reaction. Perhaps they suggest that passive income is beyond your reach and that you should just settle for a job like any "normal" person would.

It's possible these people are trying to keep you from having a failure experience, but quite often there's also some fear in the mix. What if you actually succeed? If the people around you don't have strong self-esteem, your potential success can seem threatening to them. They may expect you to fail the first time, but if you stick with it and keep going, it may worry them that the odds of success will begin to shift in your favor.

People will often try to get you to change when they sense doubt in you. When they sense certainty, they usually won't bother. So if you're getting these kinds of reactions, the most common culprit is that you're broadcasting self-doubt so loudly that other people can't help but respond to it.

Being uncertain isn't a problem, but be aware that it opens the door to being influenced. This can expose you to new ideas and suggestions, but it's hard to take action when you're in this phase because others' influences are usually not congruent with your own desires. If you stay in this uncertain phase too long, you may end up more confused and paralyzed.

When you wish to move forward with action, or if you're done spinning your wheels with doubt, then commit yourself to forward action in a particular direction. This will reduce distracting influences. If you wallow in uncertainty and keep seeking others' counsel, you'll never get anything done.

Sometimes you can find certainty through exploration, but most of the time you have to create it by choice. You never know how different decisions will turn out in advance. Just pick something and go forward anyway, like a child deciding which ride to go on first at Disneyland. You don't know if it will be the best choice, but you act like it will be the best anyway.

I often enjoy showing people around the Las Vegas Strip when they come to town. Sometimes I tell them that I'm going to show them the most amazing sight in all of Las Vegas, one they'll never be able to forget. I say this with over-the-top enthusiasm. I take them to the Bellagio Hotel, and as we turn a certain corner, I point it out to them and gasp, "Isn't this the most incredibly thing you've ever seen?" Then I show them a fountain of liquid chocolate. It's a cool thing to see if you've never seen it before, but it doesn't really live up to the hype I projected. Nevertheless, that silly enthusiasm can make the experience more fun for everyone, and it makes the experience more memorable.

You don't have to be so over-the-top in your enthusiasm for what you're doing, but if you're going to move forward in creating passive income, then create the certainty that you're on the right path, especially when you share your thoughts with others. It makes the experience more fun, and it encourages others to play back at you with their own silly enthusiasm instead of trying to get you to change their mind. It also helps to diminish potential fear or jealousy from others.

Whenever I create a new stream of passive income, I never know how it will turn out. Sometimes the results meet my expectations. Sometimes the results are better than I expected. Sometimes the results are dismal. When I'm taking action, I focus on moving forward without worrying so much about the result. I don't allow myself to be riddled with doubt and hesitation along the way since that would only lead to paralysis; it would also invite derailing influences into my life.

When other people are doubtful and hesitant, are you usually able to pick up on that? Can you tell when others are committed and when they're not?

People can sense the same in you, whether you realize it or not.

I've noticed that when I'm unsure about something I'm writing about, it opens the doors to a flood of feedback from people who want to influence me one way or the other. It also invites a lot of criticism. However, when I create more certainty in my writing, I hardly receive any feedback like that. People don't try to influence immovable objects to change.

When I first began writing about polyamory and open relationships a few years ago, I received tons of feedback about it, ranging from deeply critical to hugely supportive. I was still getting comfortable with the idea, so I still had a lot of uncertainty about it, and I'm sure that came through in my writing. It was good to invite this kind of feedback initially since it helped me think carefully about it before proceeding. But when I decided that this was the right path for me, I stopped creating and projecting doubt and uncertainty, and consequently, people stopped trying to influence my choices in this area.

If you feel that other people are trying to get you to change, and if this is becoming annoying, take a conscious look at the doubt you're projecting. People are responding to what you're broadcasting.

Many people have to deal with critical and unsupportive friends and relatives. If that's been a problem for you, then stop giving others the impression that you're uncertain and ready to waffle if they exert enough influence. You'll only bait them into trying to change your mind.

Put your attention on moving forward with action. If that's your focus, then when someone tries to influence you to stop or slow down, they won't get very far. You may choose to respond with something like, "Oh I'm sorry did you mistake me for someone who's uncertain about this? Please don't try to slow me down. I'm not interested in debating whether or not this is a good idea; I'm past that phase. I'd prefer to have your support going forward, but if you don't feel you can offer that, I understand. Just do the best you can to accept that this is important to me, even if you don't agree with it yet. If I later change my mind about this, it will be my choice to do so. But for now I'm motivated to move forward on this. Wish me luck!"

If someone tries to come over the top by brushing this off, get up and leave immediately. Don't waste your time arguing. Have enough self-respect to know that this kind of discussion is beneath you. You have every right to make your own choices. Some people can't take a hint, and you have to be assertive with them to make that clear. Sometimes it takes several confrontations before people finally see that continuing to ride you is pointless. This is especially true with relatives. It may take a few blow-offs before they can change the way they relate to you.

There's a flip side to this as well one that many people overlook. When you project uncertainty about your decisions, you not only invite criticism and derailing influences on one side, but you also repel potentially supportive influences on the other side.

If you act like you're unsure about creating passive income, then potential business partners will avoid you like the plague. Who wants to work with someone who's unsure of themselves? Who wants to risk dealing with the business-virgin?

Yes, you will build confidence through experience. But you can also create confidence by committing yourself. Either you're going to create streams of passive income, or you're not. Which will it be? It's not enough to declare that you're going to do it. If you're going to adopt a passive income lifestyle and not rely on jobs and the government to support you for the rest of your life, then start acting like it too. This includes not getting into arguments with people who either don't understand it or won't be supportive.

I remember what it was like to be just starting out on this path. My friends thought I was a bit of a slacker for not wanting a job. People would send me job applications or tell me of job openings. But when they figured out I was committed — and especially when I started making real money doing this — they all backed off. At the same time, I began attracting dozens of new entrepreneurial friends into my life, people who were much better matches for where I was at the time. With these new friends there were no pointless arguments about whether this independent path was a wise choice; that was just a given, so obvious as to be unworthy of discussion. Instead we focused on sharing ideas and supporting each others' projects.

I really do think that fear and jealousy play a part in other people's reactions. I mentioned open relationships in this article because the reactions to exploring open relationships mirror the reactions to earning passive income. Both paths involve breaking ranks with socially conditioned behaviors and embracing greater levels of abundance.

If you're still arguing and debating with people about whether or not the passive income path is a good idea, you haven't tipped yet. Those who get it know that such arguments are beneath them. When you finally see that these derailing influences are popping up in your life as a result of your own doubts and fears, I think it will help you see that in order to succeed — and especially to gain the social support you desire — you must eventually dump this limited thinking and leave it behind.

You may be wondering why I'm spending so much time on the mindset of passive income, trying to help you grasp it from different perspectives with article after article. That's because the mindset is at least 80% of the value here. Once you really understand the passive income mindset, it's all downhill from there. The action steps are easy to figure out for anyone who's committed. You can learn by trial and error, buy courses and programs and books to help you, or research ideas on the Internet. There's no need to even wait for me to finish the series.

Some people are already building new web businesses as a result of this series, and I suspect they'll be generating income before the series is over. They're taking action because they get it. Further delay is pointless. They can continue to follow this series and use it to supplement what they're learning from direct experience.

If you haven't taken any real action yet to create your first passive income stream, what's your excuse? Remember that "I Don't Know How" is not a valid excuse:

https://stevepavlina.com/blog/2012/04/i-dont-know-how-is-not-a-valid-excuse/

Other excuses for inaction are just as feeble. If you have time to read this, you have time to work on your first stream. Instead of wasting your energy on doubt and hesitation, you can make real progress by diverting that energy into forward action.

Chapter 12

Passive Value

I wanted to share this photo I took because it depicts a nice example of providing passive value.

Coming up with the idea and adding this wall art required a one-time investment of time and energy. But once it's shared, it can continue to provide value in the form of laughter and amusing conversations for visitors year after year.

Could this be monetized? Indirectly, sure. It could potentially cause more guys to talk about it . . . or to encourage their friends to use this restroom because of the silly surprise inside. Outside this restroom are several restaurants, and it's just down the hall from a big casino, which offers plenty of opportunities to spend money.

If you're curious to know, this restroom is located inside the Las Vegas Hotel (formerly known as the Las Vegas Hilton), next to their conference center. This would be one of the main restrooms used by convention-goers.

A common mistake people make in trying to creating passive income streams is that they focus on monetizing before they have anything to monetize. This is like fishing in a dry riverbed. It's wasted energy. And people do this *all the time!*

I dare say that most of the passive income failure stories I hear involve people trying to monetize a non-existent value stream. They try to go straight for the money, and their results are predictably weak. They're doing the business equivalent of begging, and so they generally earn no more than beggars do.

You can't produce a stream of passive income until you've have a stream of passive value, just as you can't catch fish until you've found some water where fish are swimming.

Focus on creating the value stream first. Then when you know you have a healthy stream going, you can work on monetizing it.

If you focus on monetization first and foremost, that's equivalent to saying, "Where are all the frakkin fish? Maybe some are hiding behind these cacti . . . or perhaps under that boulder. There must be some fish around here somewhere. Dammit, I paid good money for this fishing rod. Now, fish, listen up! I hereby command thee . . . come out from your hiding places, and skewer yourselves upon my hook!"

Stupid as this sounds, this is pretty much what people do when they get all gung ho about passive income with nary a concern for passive value.

Once you've integrated the mindset of creating passive value, and it feels like second nature to you, *then* you can think about monetizing earlier because you'll know where to look for monetization opportunities. But until that becomes a habit, I encourage you to think deliberately about creating passive value streams first, before you give any thought to monetizing them. Get good at finding water first. Then work on your fishing skills.

My challenge to you now is to do something simple that can provide some passive value for others. Remember that even a photograph can do that. Where can you share this little piece of value such that a year from now, people might still be receiving the value you provided? Don't worry about monetizing it. Just put something out there for free. Make it so.

How do you know if you're really providing value? Feedback. Your attempt is only a guess. Other people are the ultimate judges of whether or not you provided value to them.

When I saw the men's restroom mentioned above, I laughed and smiled. I snapped a photo. I shared it. For me this provided some value. If it does that for a lot of other people too, then whoever created this did a good job of creating a passive value stream.

If you do something that you believe will make people laugh, and no one laughs, then you didn't provide value. You didn't create the stream. That's okay. It happens. In your attempts to provide value, you'll often miss.

There is a skill element to value creation. It takes time to discern what people receive and appreciate as value, and it takes time to adjust your aim. I'm sure I've written many articles that few people cared about. But this helped me get better at understanding what people desire and how that matches up with what I can provide.

The more you condition this habit of looking for ways to create and provide passive value to others, the easier it will be for you to enjoy streams of passive income.

I wonder what the women's restroom looks like . . .

Chapter 13

Passive Income from Real Estate

Real estate investing is one of the most common ways that people become wealthy.

You can buy real estate such as houses, apartment buildings, office space, retail space, etc. and rent it out. You can also make money from the appreciation, assuming that real estate prices rise while you own the property.

When renting a property, it's nice if you can create a positive cashflow, meaning that your monthly rents provide enough to cover your mortgages, upkeep, property taxes, and other expenses and still leave you with some profit. Note that as you pay down the mortgages (which is essentially being done by your tenants), you will gradually own more equity in the property. You can then borrow against this equity to fund more investments, or you can sell it and cash out.

Real estate investment has some tax advantages too. One role of government is to help ensure access to housing for its citizens, and so tax laws encourage real estate development and investing.

While real estate investing can be done in ways that require a lot of cash, with some creativity you can do deals that don't require tying up a lot of money — and still generate passive income for yourself. In this capacity you can also act as a real estate dealmaker, putting deals together that other people will execute. For instance, you could assemble a proposal for a new shopping center, help get key tenants interested, and then sell the deal to a real estate developer in exchange for a cut of the revenue. This is way beyond my current expertise, but I've heard of people making good money doing these kinds of deals.

Many businesses and organizations hold a great deal of wealth in the form of real estate. For example, McDonald's not only makes money from selling dead cows; they also own many valuable street corners around the world. The Catholic Church is also a major land owner.

As your investments increase in value and your equity increases, you can borrow against your equity to buy more property, thereby increasing your holdings over time. Of course there's a risk of overextending yourself. Many real estate investors have gone bust when their over-leveraged investments sank in value, and they ended up owing more than their properties were worth while also dealing with tenants who could no longer pay the rent.

I can't share much about real estate investing since I've never been into it. I've read several books on the subject out of curiosity, but providing housing and office/retail space to tenants just doesn't excite me. I think this would be a decent way to generate passive income for someone who is patient, can be disciplined enough to stick to a long-term plan, and who knows a lot about property and is good at assessing what a property is worth.

If this type of investment interests you, please don't let my personal preferences dissuade you from investigating it fully.

Libraries have plenty of books on how to invest profitably in real estate, and I'm sure there are plenty of websites and forums where you can find good advice from experienced investors.

Even though it's not my cup of tea, I wanted to mention real estate investing as part of the passive income series since it's a common path that people use to generate passive income and long-term wealth.

Chapter 14

Virtual Real Estate

In addition to earning passive income from physical real estate, you can also generate income from virtual real estate.

Virtual real estate is online property, including domain names, websites, and online services. A virtual pub in an online game world is an example of virtual real estate.

If you've ever registered a domain name or created a website, then you've already owned some virtual real estate.

Ownership is somewhat of a gray area, both with physical and virtual real estate. I use the term loosely here. Ownership depends on how much control you have over the property, so we have a spectrum of possibilities. For instance, if you want to discover who really owns your home, stop paying your property taxes for a while and see what happens.

With virtual real estate, ownership can become especially muddled, but for the purposes of our passive income series, what we're really concerned with is how much power you have to monetize your property.

Suppose you have a Facebook page. We could say that Facebook owns it more than you do, and you don't have much control over the layout and functionality. However, you still have some ability to monetize, so you could treat it like your own virtual real estate to some extent. For example, you could recommend a product with your affiliate link, and if any of your friends buys, you earn a little money. Or you could use your Facebook page to drive traffic to your other virtual properties and then monetize that traffic.

Monetizing Virtual Real Estate

There are many ways to monetize virtual real estate, both actively and passively.

One way to make money with virtual real estate is by investing in domain names. If you can buy a domain name at one price and later sell it for more, you'll profit from the appreciation in value, and appreciation can loosely be considered a form of passive income.

I still own the domain name dexterity.com, which I've had since the mid-90s. Single-word .com domain names can be valuable these days because they're pretty much all taken (unless you invent a new word). So if I wanted to, I might be able to sell that domain for a profit.

You can also buy and sell websites, which is another way to trade in virtual real estate. Buy low, sell high, and you make a profit on the exchange. This isn't necessarily passive income, but it's a way to monetize such properties nevertheless.

Other than the value of the domain name, the value of virtual real estate depends largely on what kind of traffic it gets. More traffic is good. Higher quality traffic (meaning people who are willing to spend money) is also good.

One interesting form of virtual real estate is buying virtual property in a virtual game world. I'm not into that sort of thing, but I've heard of people making some money by buying and selling game world properties such as characters, game buildings, weapons, etc. Often they earn less than minimum wage though.

Developing Virtual Property

Anyone can buy virtual property since all you have to do is register a domain name, which can be done in minutes. This is a lot simpler than buying physical real estate.

I personally love virtual real estate since it's easy to get started, you don't need to tie up much cash, you don't have to deal with banks and title companies and mountains of fear-based paperwork, it's easy to maintain, and there are so many ways to monetize it with new ways being dreamed up every year.

I started this website for a total out of pocket cost of $9. My only expense was registering the domain name. I piggybacked the site on a web server I was using for another site, so I didn't have to pay anything extra for web hosting. After that, everything I spent to improve the website, such as software purchases and hosting upgrades, all came out of the site's revenue. Try buying physical real estate with only a $9 invest-ment. You can spend more than that on gasoline just driving around to look at properties.

My favorite way to build traffic to a website is with lots of quality free content. This attracts visitors, links, and search rankings that can help maintain and increase the value of the property over time. When my site had no traffic, I posted this free content off site, so people could actually find it. This external content then helped drive traffic to my own site.

Traffic is key. Once you have traffic, you can monetize it in so many different ways. You can sell advertising, use affiliate programs, do joint-venture deals, solicit donations, sell subscriptions to a membership site, and more. Largely this comes down to testing and experimenting. Every site is unique, so what works for one may not work for another.

Jumping on Trends

When it comes to building up virtual real estate, many people really don't know what they're doing, just as I wouldn't know what I was doing if I tried to invest in physical real estate. These people do the equivalent of trying to build a shopping mall in the middle of nowhere and then abandoning it half-finished. Then they complain that you can't make money from shopping malls.

Perhaps the biggest problem I've seen is that people try to build virtual real estate by copying what others have already done to death. You don't even want to know how many people have started personal development blogs after seeing mine. That strategy isn't going to work very well these days.

When I first launched this site in 2004, I didn't know of any other personal development bloggers. It was a relatively new idea. There were personal development experts, but they mainly focused on writing books and speaking. Most of their websites were just bare-bones online business cards, no more than 10 pages total. Many of them didn't even know what a blog was. I sensed a big opportunity there, so I jumped on it.

Seeing this opportunity in 2004 was like finding cheap, vacant land right at the edge of a rapidly growing metropolitan area. You know that as the city grows, that land is going to become increasingly valuable, so it's a wise investment.

When I started in 2004, for me and other bloggers like me, it was almost like we could do no wrong. There was far more demand for blogs than bloggers could satisfy. Many other bloggers who started around that time saw their traffic grow like gangbusters. Those golden days are over.

If I was starting out today, I would *not* start a personal development blog. This field is way too crowded in the blogosphere now. It would be a major uphill climb against entrenched competition to stand out, build a following, and get to the top of the search engines. I'm not saying it's impossible to succeed with a new blog now — it can still be done — but it's not nearly as accessible as it once was. There are much easier targets.

If I was starting out today and wanted to work in essentially the same field, I'd go where there's still a lot of empty real estate, and I could get in cheap and build a following. I might get into ebooks since that market is exploding due to all the iPad sales, and it's nowhere near the saturation point yet.

Other good choices would be apps for iPhones, iPads, and Android Tablets and phones. Another option would be to develop apps for Chrome, which recently became the #1 browser. And since the new Macbook Pro came out this week, you might develop a new app to take advantage of the Retina display as well as some of the new features of OS X Mountain Lion, which launches next month. Some of these markets may seem crowded already, but I think we're just getting started.

Back in 2004 I was worried that I might be getting into blogging late because there were already 8 million blogs when I started, although most were akin to personal journals. Now there are probably 400-500 million blogs. I think we'll see the same explosion in ebooks and various app markets over the next few years. You think 650,000 iPhone/iPad apps is a lot? Wait a few years. This is still early.

As Wayne Gretzky would say, skate where the puck is going, not where it's been. Blogs are yesterday's news. If you haven't already ridden that wave to the top by now, you've missed the boat. Focus on the newer, more recent opportunities that are just emerging but that aren't so saturated with competition yet.

When it comes to online real estate, if you snooze, you lose. When you see an opportunity, act on it.

Overcoming Excuses

One of the reasons people hesitate to take action is that they drown themselves in excuses. People who succeed could use all the same excuses though. It's not the existence of potential excuses that's the problem. It's the willingness to succumb to them.

As I noted in a previous article, "I don't know how" is perhaps the biggest and lamest excuse of all.

If you don't know how, do it anyway. Once you do it, then you'll know how. Of course you're never going to know how the first time. Nobody does.

People often think they're supposed to succeed with a process like this:

1. Set a goal.

2. Figure out how to accomplish it in a step by step manner.

3. Follow the steps to complete the goal.

When they can't complete step 2, they get stuck and procrastinate. They also whine a lot, which I hate.

A more realistic approach looks something like this:

1. Set a goal.

2. Figure out one small action that might move you closer to that goal. Worst case, just guess.

3. Take that action from step 2.

4. If you haven't accomplished the goal yet, repeat from step 2.

Last year I didn't know how to create a song. I didn't know what the steps were. I couldn't use the first method. But I was able to complete a song using the second method. I could guess at the first step, which was to run GarageBand on my Mac for the first time. Once the program was running and I looked at the interface, I had some ideas for what the next action step might be, such as "Create New Project." Within that same session, I created my first song. It was awful and only 12 seconds long, but it got me started. And within a week or so, I was able to create something that was about 3 minutes long and at least tolerable.

It's the same thing with building virtual real estate. No one knows how to do it at first, but they do it anyway. You just guess at a step and do it. Then you guess at another step and do it. Keep adapting and acting till you get somewhere interesting.

If you think you need to know all the action steps before you start, you're just being goofy and paranoid. Even if someone else gives you the action steps that worked for them, they probably won't work quite the same for you. The inputs will be different. You can try following a recipe, but it will come out a little differently each time.

Don't psyche yourself out before you begin. With any sort of passive income stream, you'll learn as you go. To a newbie that may seem like a scary thought. But once you get used to it, you'll see that the uncertainty is what makes it fun.

Chapter 15

Generating Ideas

As we go through this passive income series, you may start getting ideas for how you can create new streams of passive income. How do you know which ideas are worth pursuing?

Keep It Simple

It's easy to bite off more than you can chew with your first passive income idea. If you already have a track record of successfully completing large projects, then don't let me stop you. But if you have a tendency to get discouraged and give up too soon, I suggest scaling down your ambitions. Start small by tackling a simple project that you're confident you can actually complete.

It's better to complete a 30-page ebook and sell it for $7 and generate a few sales per month than it is to tackle a 200-page writing project and never get it done. The former provides some genuine value to people; the latter will merely frustrate you.

Treat your early projects as training for your success muscles. The greatest predictor of future success is actually past success, so think about creating some simple successes by taking on modest projects and getting them done and released. Once you've done a few of those, then consider scaling up and tackling bigger projects. Even with seemingly simple projects, you're going to learn a lot. You'll get faster, and then it will be easier to scale up and tackle larger projects.

It's so easy to underestimate how long things will take by overlooking details. With some of my early game projects, I'd estimate that I could crank out a particular arcade-style game in 2-3 weeks, but in reality it would take me 6 months. There are so many hidden steps that are easy to gloss over with an off-the-cuff estimate, such as creating the installation program, creating the music and sound effects, writing the documentation, setting up the online ordering system, etc.

If you've never created a passive income stream before, your first project may involve lots of one-time steps like setting up an online shopping cart. But once you've done that initial setup work, you can create similar streams with greater ease simply by plugging them into the same system.

Try not to get overly excited about making a killing with your first passive income project. Put your attention on learning the ropes and generate a nice little stream. Then you can scale up by creating more streams. If you can generate even $50 a month with your first stream, I'd say you're off to a good start. It's generally harder to go from $0 to $50 a month than it is to go from $50 to $500 per month.

Inspiration vs. Market Research

There are two main schools of thought on how to pick income-producing creative projects. One is to go with your gut and do whatever inspires you. If you get an idea for a new project, run with it right away. The other idea is to research what people actually want to buy and then create something for that target market. This is the classic "find a need and fill it approach."

I tend to get the best results by combining both approaches. First, I saturate myself in trying to understand what people want. I can do this via online research, surveys, or just talking to people. Over the years I've met hundreds of my blog readers face to face, especially at workshops, so that helps me better understand their needs and what I can provide that will be helpful to them.

If you have your own website or existing audience that you can use for market research, that's a great place to start, but you can just as easily gather information from other websites.

When I was creating computer games, I started out by making simple arcade games because those were relatively easy to design and create. My games didn't sell well though. So I did some market research, looking for where there was strong demand for new games from customers, especially in genres that I was interested in. I spent hours on game download sites (where game developers would post their free demos), observing which categories got the most downloads. I downloaded dozens of demos to get a sense of what else was out there, how popular various games were, and what I might be able to contribute that would be unique enough but also familiar enough to sell well.

That's when I settled on making a cerebral puzzle game.

The low end market for puzzle games was very crowded, especially with match-3 types of games, but I could see that the smarter end of the puzzle game market was underserved at the time, yet there was still some decent demand. People were downloading a lot of so-so games in that category. So this research helped me realize that if I made a decent game in that category, it would probably sell well.

I think this type of mental saturation was a good place to begin because it helped me narrow my focus, so generating ideas wasn't an overwhelming task. I could then think about creating something in one of the sub-genres where I perceived good opportunities.

After that I began brainstorming some potential design ideas. I find that taking in a lot of input really helps when it comes to generating ideas. When I do this, I notice gaps in other people's creations that help me see where I could take things in a different direction, thereby contributing something unique.

Once I had an idea that inspired me, it still took a lot of work to implement it. To create that game took about 4 months of solid design effort just to create a 5-page design document. Everything else — programming, artwork, music, sound effects, level design, testing, and release — took another 2 months. In its first month on the market, this new game sold more than my previous 4 games combined, and several months later it was earning 10 times what the other games were earning. That's the power of market research. If you sell something people actually want to buy, you can do a lot better financially.

How to Do Market Research

I'm not really too particular about how I conduct market research. There are so many variables that you can get bogged down in analysis paralysis if you overdo it. I take a pretty light-weight approach to it.

Mainly I look for two things:

1. What are people already buying?

2. Where are there gaps with relatively high demand and low supply that I could potentially serve?

Sometimes it's hard to answer #1 directly because you probably don't have access to other people's sales figures. But you can often use other public data to make some educated guesses. I didn't know other game developers' sales figures, but I could go to download sites and see how many downloads each demo had and how many games there were in each category. I could then calculate average downloads for each game in a a particular category. If I saw that one category had triple per game downloads of another category, well it wasn't hard to surmise that one genre might make me triple the sales of another genre.

I could also look up traffic rankings for a developers' website to see how popular it was (such as with Alexa.com). And I knew many developers personally, so I had a general sense of who was making money and who wasn't. All of this information combined to give me a decent idea of where there was good money to be earned and where there wasn't.

During the late 1990s and early 2000s, I could see that developers of casual games were typically doing pretty well. Friends were making six figures a year selling card games and puzzle games. Today those markets are even bigger, especially with the expansion of tablet and cell phone games.

It can be a tricky balancing act between making something that inspires you and making something that people want to buy. There's surely some luck and randomness involved too. But I've seen situations where results are 10, 20, or 50 times better when creators finally agree to give customers what they want instead of trying to convince customers to want what's been created.

Do I think you should sacrifice your artistic integrity to satisfy the public? No, I don't think it's necessary to do that. I think most people who feel they must choose one or the other are creating a false dichotomy due to limiting beliefs and blocks to making good money. I didn't feel I had to sacrifice my art to please others. In fact, I felt that paying more attention to what other people wanted made me a better artist. I liked having more customers to appreciate my creations.

If you think you have to choose one or the other, I encourage you to question whether that's really true. Can you take the pulse of what other people want to buy and then focus on pursuing inspired ideas that will land somewhere in the general vicinity? I think that's doable.

Much of the time when artists claim to be undiscovered geniuses and lament that they can't make money doing what they love, I think the likely truth is that their art just isn't very good yet.

I think some of the best art is developed with a strong social component, meaning that there's ongoing feedback between the artist and the patrons.

Making Reasonable Trade-offs

Another advantage to knowing what people want is that you know when you're going against those desires to some extent, and you can make this choice consciously without any self-delusion.

Based on surveys I had done, I expected that the *Conscious Success Workshop* would sell a lot better than the *Conscious Relationships Workshop* earlier this year. And that is of course what happened. CSW got twice as many registrations as CRW.

I could predict in advance that I'd earn more money doing something other than a relationships workshop. I accepted that, and I still felt inspired to do such a workshop, even knowing that the decision would mean earning less money. I felt that a smaller group would be better for this topic since it would be more intimate.

So in this case, the research gave me an idea of what to expect. I could make an informed choice, and there wouldn't be any disappointment with the lower sales.

It's nice to get an idea of what the trade-offs are when you put other concerns ahead of making money. Then you can ask yourself if the freedom to create what you desire is worth the financial impact. There's no right or wrong way to make these decisions. It's a matter of personal preference. You can make different choices over time and see how each type of project plays out.

Taking Risks

With new and untested ideas, there's always some risk involved, but everyone has a different level of risk tolerance.

If you're less risk tolerant, then I would put more effort into market research, so you do a better job of aiming where the demand is. That way you don't waste your time creating something that no one wants to buy.

If you're more risk tolerant, you can take the chance of doing something new where it's hard to conduct market research. Success is far from guaranteed, but you might just stumble upon some previously unknown demand.

This is a matter of personal choice, and your preferences may change depending on what else is going on in your life. It's like any form of investing. Do you want to play it safe and deal with relatively predictable outcomes, or do you want to take a chance and explore uncharted territory?

Both Site Build-It and the Getting Rich With Ebooks program I mentioned earlier explain how to conduct online research using various tools in their specific domains. So SBI provides tools to help you see where there's good potential to create a money-making website, and GRWE helps you research potential topics for ebooks where you can expect good sales.

That said, if you're more of a risk taker, you can bypass these tools and go with whatever inspires you. You might hit upon something new that works, but you could just as easily end up with a total dud. Who would ever want to do that? I sometimes like doing that. It can be exciting to try something new and see what happens, assuming you can handle it if it doesn't work out so well. This is especially doable for small projects where the downside isn't so terrible if it doesn't perform.

Since I have enough streams of passive income to support me,

I can afford to take more chances with new income streams. But if I was just starting out, I might be more conservative and make sure I'm tackling projects where I can predict strong demand.

A lot of this research can be done with free tools and public information. For example, you can see how well any book is selling relative to any other book by checking the sales rankings on Amazon.com. For all kinds of products now, you can get a decent idea of how well any particular product is selling just by looking at public data. This is not difficult if you have decent Internet skills.

Inspiration First

Sometimes I get inspired ideas before I've done any market research. In those cases I can still do some research after the fact to validate or invalidate the idea. Maybe I'm excited about it in the moment, but the question is: Will it sell?

For instance, a few years ago I got the idea to offer personal coaching, but I didn't know exactly what to offer or what to charge for it. It felt like an inspired idea that I should pursue, but I had a lot of uncertainty about it. So I decided to do a test by offering a 1-hour consultation on eBay and inviting people to bid on it.

The auction reached $1,000 before eBay pulled the plug and killed it. Apparently eBay doesn't let you offer intangible items for sale. Generally they do a poor job of enforcing this policy since there were plenty of other intangible items listed, but my auction was probably a bit too high profile to duck under their radar.

Fortunately the auction lasted long enough to convince me

that there would likely be some decent demand for coaching, so I began offering that service. I don't promote it much because I know it's beyond the price range of most people, but it's there for those who want it.

So this was an example of how the inspiration came first, and then I did a little research and testing to validate it a bit more before committing to it.

As another example of this, I'm in the process of booking a new 3-day workshop in Las Vegas. This one will be unlike anything I've done before. It will have no set topic, no pre-planned content, no pre-arranged exercises, and no written materials or handouts. This will be an experiment in co-creating a transformational experience with the audience. Our challenge will be to go with the flow of inspiration the whole way through — and still to make it an engaging, growth-stimulating experience for those who attend.

So this will be a workshop where we'll have a lot more flexibility. I'll be facilitating it, but I won't wield such tight control over how it turns out as I have at previous workshops. It's going to be a balancing act to keep us in the sweet spot of creating inspired growth experiences without descending into chaos.

At the January CSW workshop, someone asked me to share a goal or project that I felt would challenge me, and I shared the basic idea for this workshop. Then I quickly dismissed it as impractical. *But who'd actually want to go to a workshop like that?* I said. It seemed like it would be an interesting experience for me as a speaker, but I couldn't imagine too many people wanting to sign up for it, especially since I couldn't realistically tell them what to expect.

But someone replied, "I'd actually go to that." Then someone else said "Yeah, that sounds like fun." A quick survey revealed that about 2/3 of the people in the room were interested in attending such a workshop. I was shocked that so many people resonated with the idea. It always sounded like a crazy idea to me. That got me thinking about it more seriously. *Could I actually do this?*

For additional validation, I talked to some speaker friends about this idea, and a couple of them told me, "Yeah, I did a workshop like that before." I asked them how it went, and each of them said something like, "Best workshop I ever did. People loved it!" They told me that the spontaneity of it made it work very well. They also pointed out that the people who are willing to attend such a workshop are the kinds of people who will ensure its success; it attracts people who can help co-create a cool experience for everyone.

After a few more conversations about the idea, I finally decided to go for it. It's a risk because I really don't know how to sell a workshop with no set topic, where we'll be going with the flow of whatever inspires us in the moment. Part of me still thinks it's a crazy idea, but this is another case where I feel the coolness factor of doing something new outweighs the certainty of having semi-predictable sales. For all I know, the idea might turn out to be a homerun. The only way to know is to try.

This is actually another way to conduct market research. Dive in and test your idea in the real world. Then you'll know. The benefit to this approach is that you might just stumble upon something that works really well. Then you can build around it.

The Courage Advantage

If you're more courageous than most people, your courage can give you a serious advantage because it cuts down on competition. One reason public speaking pays so well is that so many people are afraid of it, so it's not as competitive as other fields. So if you're willing to go where others are afraid to go, most of your would-be competitors will surrender those markets to you.

So to summarize the ideas in this article, idea selection has a lot to do with risk tolerance. The less risk tolerant you are, the more you'll want to rely on market research and assessing demand to guide your decisions. As your risk tolerance increases, you can afford to take on projects that rely more heavily on going with the flow of inspiration, but even in those cases, you may still choose to validate them with a little market research to give you enough confidence to get moving.

If you're going to go through the trouble of creating something of value to share with people, I think it's reasonable to do at least a modest amount of market research to get a general sense of what you can expect income-wise, even if income generation is just one concern among many.

What if you can't come up with any ideas at all? Try ordering a quad shot latte — that should get a few ideas flowing.

A good article to read to help counter-balance the points in this article would be my post "What Are the Odds of Becoming a Black Belt?"

https://stevepavlina.com/blog/2006/12/what-are-the-odds-of-becoming-a-black-belt/

This will help you avoid some of the pitfalls of market research, such as getting bogged down in thinking about your odds of success instead of actually placing bets on the choicest opportunities.

Chapter 16

Fame

Fame is attention. With enough attention you can generate passive income.

Monetizing Fame

Monetizing fame is actually pretty easy. Consider the Oprah effect. When Oprah recommends a book, it sells like crazy. If she wanted to, she could leverage her fame to promote products, businesses, and more in exchange for a cut of the sales. Lots of companies would be happy to pay her for an endorsement.

The Catholic Church is excellent at leveraging fame to make money. The Church has many supporters who go out of their way to market it. This generates new subscribers who are in turn encouraged to go out and spread the "good news." By taking the form of a non-profit, they also avoid many taxes. L. Ron Hubbard copied their model to create the Church of Scientology, which is also quite wealthy.

Celebrities commonly generate income streams by endorsing products and services. With enough leverage they can be granted a cut of the sales they help generate, stock options, and additional perks. Their endorsement may not involve much direct effort, maybe a photo shoot or some filming, but it can produce significant income if the celebrity's recommendation carries a lot of weight in terms of generating sales.

Many celebrities have millions of Twitter followers, even though they often share mostly personal updates that no one would ever want to read if it came from a non-celeb. With such large audiences, they could recommend all kinds of things that make them money, such as William Shatner did by appearing in Priceline commercials. Movie stars can promote their own movies too, which puts more money in their pockets if they can help sell more movie tickets.

Fame provides many benefits because attention begets more attention. A famous movie star gets more movie offers because the star's fame can drive more people to see the movie. More movies mean even more fame and recognition.

You don't have to become a major movie star to enjoy some of the benefits of fame. Even a little fame can help. For instance, due to the popularity of my website, I've been quoted in the New York Times three times. My website has been mentioned in quite a few books as well as on TV. I've never paid for any of this extra publicity. More exposure can generate more web traffic, and that's something I already know how to monetize. I don't have a good way to measure how much this helps income-wise, but I'm sure it has some effect.

You have to be careful when monetizing fame because there's always a chance of killing the goose that lays the golden eggs. If you do something stupid that kills your reputation and turns everyone against you, your fame will become infamy. Interestingly, you can still monetize infamy, but you may need to use different strategies. The greater risk to your financials is muddying your reputation and being forgotten.

Public vs. Private Life

Some famous people are really into brand and reputation management. Quite often their real lives differ significantly from their public personas, but they keep playing up those personas, partly because it makes them money. One of the best examples of this would be pro wrestling, where the public characters can be so bizarre and conflict-driven. Drama sells more tickets.

When I realized that my web traffic was likely to give me a small dose of online celebrity, I made a conscious choice that I didn't want to have to manage two different characters in my psyche. Whether in public or private, I do my best to behave the same way and not to hide aspects of my personality, regardless of how people may judge me. But many people don't feel good about doing this, so they separate their public and private selves.

Whether you invent a public character to portray or do your best to be your same self in both worlds is a matter of personal preference. However, you can run into problems when you pretend that your public persona is your real private self as well. Many speakers have fallen into this trap.

How to Become Famous

How do you become famous in the first place? I'd say the #1 rule is to violate expectations. Fame is attention, and to get attention you need to stand out. Copying what everyone else does only makes you invisible. To become famous you must do something exceptional, unusual, or extraordinary. Flaunt your uniqueness. Learn what other people did to become famous, and then discard their solutions and do something different. It's okay to model someone's general approach, but don't copy their personal style or technique unless you want to be labeled "So and so, junior."

I gained some degree of fame by publicly sharing so many of my interests on my blog, including my experiments in polyphasic sleep and raw foods, my interest in open relationships and D/s play and threesomes, my explorations of subjective reality, etc. Of course there are many people who share these interests, so I'm not particularly unique in that regard. But not many people were willing to share such details in public, especially people in the personal development field. Writers in this field had a tendency to whitewash their lives and present a sanitized public image. I shared the more experimental side of my life, and when I did so, people would thank me for it. People with similar interests or challenges could relate to what I was going through and learn from my failures and successes. They encouraged me to continue. I also felt good about doing this.

I recognized early on that if I kept up this approach, it would surely turn some people against me, such as people who get upset by articles like 10 Reasons You Should Never Have a Religion or How to Graduate From Christianity, but on balance I've gained much more traffic and income than I've lost by writing on such topics openly. In some media this would backfire, but with blogging people tend to place more value on honesty and authenticity than on needing the writer to clone their values.

Fame is a mixed bag. While it can open up a lot of doors, it can also do weird things to your social life. If you can feel congruent with this path, it's not that difficult to become famous. The hard part is reaching the point where you can accept and welcome the whole package. Most people could appreciate the benefits of fame but definitely wouldn't want to deal with the drawbacks such as the loss of privacy, endless solicitations, and the public criticism they'd have to deal with, and so they reject the package as a whole; this virtually ensures they won't become famous.

Even the people I know who seem pretty comfortable with fame still generally keep it at arms length as much as possible. For them fame is a byproduct of pursuing other interests, but it's not a particularly worthy end in itself.

Chapter 17

Donations

One of the simplest ways to start earning passive income right away is to request donations. Just invite people to give you money.

The Kindness of Strangers

In rare situations donations can really take off. Consider the recent case of Karen Klein, the New York bus monitor who was filmed being bullied by students on the bus. A guy named Max Sidorov started a campaign to raise money for her to take a vacation, via the site Indiegogo, with a goal of raising $5,000.

As the abuse video went viral, racking up millions of views on YouTube, and news of this campaign spread, donation pledges came pouring in. Last time I checked, Karen's donations were well in excess of $500,000, and there are still 28 days left in the fundraising campaign.

On top of that, someone started an Indiegogo campaign to raise some "love money" for Max as well, perhaps to reward him for coming up with the idea. The initial goal was to raise $2,500 for Max, and that campaign is already past $4,400.

Before this is over, Karen Klein could very well be a millionaire. And she didn't even ask for this.

Apparently Karen's normal salary as a bus monitor was $15K per year. At the rate her donations are increasing, she's probably earning a year's salary in a few hours now.

Ask and It Is Given

My results with donations are nowhere near as explosive as Karen's, but I do invite and accept donations as one of many passive income streams. Donations are one of my smallest streams, but they can add up over time, and this stream is very easy to maintain.

I first began testing donations in 2005. I'd been blogging for several months but wasn't really making money at it. I started getting emails from people telling me they wanted to pay me something for all the value they'd received from my free content. One of them asked if he could PayPal me some money. I said sure, and he gave me a donation.

Others encouraged me to make it easier for them to donate, and taking their advice actually saved me time. Otherwise people would have kept asking. So I put up a donations page with a PayPal link. PayPal can automatically generate the HTML code and donation button for you, so this is very easy to do.

The amount of money I've made from donations has varied over time. At its peak several years ago, I would see $1-2K in donations per month. These days it's around $500-700 per month on average. Although it's not a major income stream, donations still bring in thousands of dollars in income per year.

If you already have a website that provides some decent value for free, I encourage you to at least try putting up a donations link and see what happens. If at least a few people want to pay you back in some small way, why not make it easy for them?

I've received many donations for $100, $200, and even $300+. It's nice to receive this extra financial support, especially when providing so much content for free.

Effectiveness of Donations

Donations help, but I wouldn't suggest basing your entire income strategy around donations unless you're creating a non-profit enterprise and you have someone in charge of fundraising, or if you have a truly massive audience like Wikipedia. For a normal web business, donations can provide a nice little income stream, but I wouldn't count on them to cover all of your expenses.

On the other hand, if you have the ability to create a major viral campaign around your fundraising efforts like Max Sidorov did for Karen Klein, then a donation-centric strategy may be worth a try.

If you want to start generating some passive income, meet the universe halfway. Ask!

Chapter 18

Why Ebooks Are Such a Golden Opportunity

Recent data from 1189 publishers shows that ebook sales have overtaken hardcover book sales and will overtake paperback books soon.

In comparing the same sales period for 2011 vs. 2012, hardcover sales increased by 2. 7% while ebook sales increased by 28. 1%. It's difficult for the supply of quality ebook offerings to keep up with this kind of growth rate, so ebook sellers are likely to see stronger than normal demand for their existing ebooks for quite a while.

Paperback books are still #1 in terms of sales, but this lead isn't expected to last much longer.

One category in particular that's been skyrocketing (both for ebook and hardcover sales) is young adult and children's books. This genre has been seeing triple digit growth rates.

As I mentioned in a previous post about passive income systems, the data clearly points to some major opportunities for selling ebooks.

What's driving this rapid growth in ebook sales? Tablet computers and ebook reading devices like the iPad and Kindle.

Tablet Computers Driving Ebook Sales

Let's take a quick look at the projections for tablet sales.

Deutsche Bank projects that 97 million tablet computers will ship in 2012, increasing to 124 million in 2013. That would be a 28% increase year over year. This isn't for the same year as the ebook sales, but does this number look familiar?

iPad sales alone are expected to pass 60 million units in 2012, increasing to 74 million in 2014.

Even Microsoft has broken with its previous business model, bypassing its hardware partners to create its own tablet hardware, called Microsoft Surface. The tablet space is clearly heating up with competition. Billions of dollars worth of tablet computers are being sold every month now.

Most of these tablet devices are geared for consuming content rather than for creating content. This is creating a big surge in demand for apps, games, and of course ebooks.

A Golden Opportunity for Ebook Authors

These numbers suggest some major opportunities for ebook authors. It's really not that difficult to create and sell an ebook these days, even if you've never written one before. A good place to start is Vic Johnson's program that teaches you how to create and sell ebooks; his intro video also shares more data about why this is an unusually good time to sell ebooks. Vic even shares contact info for the vendors he uses, so you can get help formatting your ebook, creating a nice cover for it, and so on.

I spoke to Vic again last week, and he noted that it's very doable to create decent passive income streams just by focusing on the three major players (Amazon, Apple/iBooks, and Barnes&Noble/Nook). It's great if you have a website to sell your ebooks too, but these days that isn't necessary. My book *Personal Development for Smart People* was published by Hay House in 2008, and it has ebook versions for the Kindle, iBooks, etc., but I don't sell any copies directly through my website.

I'm most likely going to create and sell an ebook for the walk-through I do later in this passive income series. The writing on the wall is too clear to ignore. This is a juicy opportunity that isn't going to last forever. With the rapid growth of ebook and tablet computer sales, this is a great time to get into ebooks. It's possible to see increasing sales for a while just from watching the market expand. This reminds me of the opportunity I saw in 2004 when I started blogging; many bloggers were able to see significant traffic increases from the general expansion of the blogosphere.

I'm planning to stick with nonfiction since that's my strength, but there are some serious opportunities if you think you can crank out a kid's or young adult book. Teens and tweens just can't get enough of those vampire stories!

Vic also generously offered to help out with some additional Q&A since he can see that hundreds of people from my website are currently taking his course (I expect it to get into the thousands as we continue this series). He suggested that we invite people to send us their questions about creating and selling ebooks. Vic and I will select about 10 questions and have a phone conversation to discuss and answer them, record the call, and share it here. So if you have a question you'd like to submit to us, especially one you feel isn't already answered by Vic's program, feel free to send it to me.

https://stevepavlina.com/contact/

I'm really looking forward to going through this process myself. On the one side, I enjoy teaching people about passive income, and I have about 17 years of experience making money this way, so there's plenty to share. On the other side, I also love trying new things since I get bored easily if I keep doing the same thing over and over. While Vic has created and sold many ebooks very successfully (earning more than $7 million from ebooks), I've barely dabbled in this. It's going to be fun!

As a final piece of advice, try not to get so worked about about whether or not your first income stream is a homerun vs. a flop. Passive income is a skill to develop for the long run. The only way to really know how well a given idea works is to test it. You can do some market research to put the odds in your favor, such as Vic explains how to do in his program, but it also helps if you can go into this with a beginner's mind and stay open to all possible outcomes without succumbing to feelings of neediness and desperation. I found it especially helpful to adopt this attitude when I was just starting out.

Chapter 19

Investing

Another way to earn passive income is through investing. I've already mentioned real estate investing, but of course you can also generate income from many other types of investments such as owning stock in a company or earning interest with a certificate of deposit.

Investments can pay off with interest, dividends, and capital gains. Depending on the current tax laws and how much you're earning, your investment gains may also be subjected to lower taxes than other forms of income, partly because governments want to encourage more economic growth.

Here are some general assessments to make with regards to different investments:

Facts – What are the specific details of the investment? For businesses this is called *fundamental analysis*. Look at the current state of the business, including its physical property, technology, intellectual property, cash, cashflow, debt, and industry conditions. This helps you evaluate the investment relative to other potential investments.

Performance – If this is a pre-existing investment, you can look at its past performance. While past performance can't predict the future accurately, it's an indicator of where things are headed. *Technical analysis* is an approach to investing that looks at past performance metrics to assess the likelihood that an investment will increase in value.

Risk – How risky is the investment? Does it seem fairly stable, or has it been experiencing high volatility?

Return – What is the expected rate of return? Do you anticipate a reasonable payoff relative to your investment and the perceived risk?

Control – How much control do you personally wield over this investment? If you buy common stock in a company, you may be able to exert a small degree of influence as a stockholder. If you sit on the Board of Directors, you can exert more influence. And if you're the CEO, you can exert even more influence. This is a mixed blessing. More control means you have more abilities to steer your investments, but it also means you bear more responsibility if things go south.

Impact – Are you investing to make as much money as possible, or are you responsibly contributing through your investments? Where you invest your money, time, and energy will impact how you feel about yourself as well as how you influence the overall economy. Will you invest in weapons, junk food, soda, drugs, oil drilling, cosmetics, banking, entertainment, gambling, pesticides, cigarettes, factory farming, etc? If you put money in an S&P 500 index fund, you're supporting all of these things and more. See for yourself where your money is going.

I tend to put a lot of weight on that last factor when considering investments. For this reason I even regard charitable donations as a form of investment. I may not see a financial return from those outlays, but I can still contribute to the impact.

If you try to invest from a place that doesn't align with your values, you'll probably end up sabotaging yourself. In the past I owned some mutual funds, but I dumped them many years ago. I prefer not to directly support companies like Monsanto, McDonald's, and Philip Morris in pursuing goals that seem so out of alignment with my values.

My favorite places to invest are: (1) in my own personal growth, and (2) in my own business. Investing in personal growth means paying for growth-inducing experiences like books, audio programs, courses, seminars, coaching, training, travel, and more — anything that helps you grow. See my post "The Best Place to Invest Your Money" for details:

https://stevepavlina.com/blog/2005/02/the-best-place-to-invest-your-money/

Investing in a business that you own can help make the business more stable, so you can enjoy passive income from it for years or decades to come.

Some people confuse trading with long-term investing. Trading is closer to active income, whereby you buy and sell quickly and repeatedly, making gains on these exchanges. Even if you do well with trading, your income stops when you aren't actively working. Long-term investing is a more passive approach, whereby you do most of your work up front to select good investments, then (hopefully) watch them increase in value with minimal maintenance on your part. If you're checking on a stock price every day, that isn't particularly passive.

While the admonition "it takes money to make money" can

apply to investing, there's still plenty of room for people who can skillfully invest other people's money, sharing in the gains. Whether you have money to invest or not, some degree of skill is important, either skill at picking investments or at picking investment advisors. These skills can of course be developed over time, regardless of your starting point.

I can't personally advise you much on becoming a pro investor since it hasn't been a serious interest of mine. I feel it's important to mention it in this series for the sake of thoroughness, but if this is your preferred vehicle, you'll need to seek out other resources for more specific help.

The main contribution I want to make here is to encourage you to think carefully about the long-term impact of your investments on the world as a whole. You'll find it much easier to invest in alignment with your values since you won't be fighting a part of yourself (i.e. less self-sabotage). The good news is that there's still plenty of money to be made from intelligent investments that create positive ripples for others. There's no need to settle for harmful investments that violate your values and leave you feeling conflicted and incongruent.

Chapter 20

Dissolving Limiting Beliefs

As one of our final stops before we do the passive income walkthrough, I want to address limiting beliefs, which could seriously hold you back from achieving your goals if we don't take steps to address them.

Types of Limiting Beliefs

Limiting beliefs come in a variety of forms. Here are some of the most common.

If-then beliefs

- If I try to start a new passive income stream, I'll fail, and that would be bad.

- If I express interest in someone, I'll get rejected.

- If I succeed in a big way, my friends won't like me as much.

Universal Beliefs

- People are inherently selfish.

- Children always misbehave.

- Money is the root of all evil.

Personal and Self-Esteem Beliefs

- I'm not good enough.

- I don't matter.

- I'm not lovable.

How Limiting Beliefs Show Up

Limiting beliefs are usually subconscious. They operate below the level of awareness most of the time. You'll typically notice them by their side effects first, often when setting ambitious goals and trying to pursue them.

Suppose you want to create your first stream of passive income. If you've been following this series since April, then you've already set a goal with a specific dollar amount. Maybe you're aiming for $100/month for your first stream.

Now if we look at this from a strictly objective perspective, this is an achievable goal. There's nothing spectacular, miraculous, or magical about it. It's been done many times before, and in certain circles it's a rather mundane and commonplace event. This goal is not a special snowflake.

But how many people who set this goal will actually achieve it? Is there some doubt as to whether you'll be one of those who'll succeed?

Many people are in fact going to succeed. For many of them, however, it won't be a smooth ride. They'll succeed not because their ideas are any better or their passion is any greater than most. They'll succeed because they're willing to change their beliefs and self-image to align with their goals instead of letting their past mental patterns get in the way of their goals.

A significant part of this shift in thinking involves letting go of mental clutter in the form of limiting beliefs. With the passive income series, you may encounter beliefs within yourself such as:

- It's too hard to earn passive income.

- I'm supposed to go out and get a real job.

- I'm not smart enough to make this work.

- Passive income is too strange for me.

- I should just do what everyone else does.

- Having a regular job is safe and secure.

Many people who succeed in creating passive income streams start out with limiting beliefs like these. After all, it's how modern society conditions us to think.

When you start working on a new goal, your limiting beliefs will rarely express themselves openly. Usually they'll show up by influencing your thinking and behaviors in ways that tear you away from your goal, effectively starving it of attention.

For instance, you'll start thinking about passive income ideas, and as soon as you come up with a decent idea, your mind will begin coming up with reasons why it won't work. You'll talk yourself out of it.

Or you'll share your idea with your most pessimistic friend, subconsciously knowing that your friend will try to talk you out of it. You could have shared the idea with your most optimistic friend instead, who may have encouraged you to go for it.

Or you'll begin working on your idea, and suddenly you'll be struck by the irresistible urge to go out and see a movie or buy a new game.

Or you'll allocate a few hours to work on your goal, and somehow those hours will get chewed up by web surfing or perhaps some unexpected crisis like, "Oh no we seem to be out of chocolate! Guess I'd better head to the store This goal stuff will have to wait a bit longer."

You've consciously decided that the goal is important to you, but you can observe the pattern that your mind isn't fully cooperating with you. It keeps nudging you towards distractions when you need to get some real work done.

The culprit in such situations is quite often limiting beliefs.

Why Do We Have Limiting Beliefs?

Many limiting beliefs are installed in early childhood, and they do serve a purpose of sorts. They act as mental shortcuts to keep us safe. But the downside is that our brains overgeneralize in these cases, installing patterns that overlook subtle nuances. Hence these patterns are often inaccurate. But to manage our survival, they don't need to be perfectly accurate. They just need to be good enough, especially when fast decisions are required.

Partly this is due to how our brains evolved, with our human neocortex wrapped around the much more ancient limbic brain. The limbic brain handles our emotions, behavior, motivation, and long-term memory. The neocortex handles conscious thought, higher reasoning, and language.

These different brain areas evolved to help us survive, but many goals are not necessary for survival. Passive income certainly isn't. Your brain isn't naturally wired by default to help you achieve your passive income goal. But fortunately your brain is very flexible and can learn to cooperate with this goal.

When we tackle certain non-survival goals, we can't simply rely on our default mental programming. That programming is good enough to keep us alive, but more often than not, it doesn't perform very well when it comes to loftier ambitions. So we need to refine this programming in some areas, tweaking it to remove unnecessary limitations. We don't want our brains to trigger a fear response, for instance, when we want to switch careers. We want to be able to make sensible decisions based on our knowledge and skills, not on emotional triggers from childhood.

For instance, can you get up on a stage and do public speaking without suffering undue nervousness? Can you comfortable speak off the cuff in front of a group even if you haven't prepared anything? If you can't do that, it's because your limbic brain is triggering fear and danger signals that are paralyzing you. Physically you could do it since all you need to do is get up and talk. Speaking is just talking. It's really not that complicated.

Similarly, can you go create a new stream of passive income if that's what you want? The action steps are pretty easy. But will your limbic brain, in charge of emotion and motivation, cooperate with your decision? You may often find that it won't. It triggers a phantom threat to your survival and makes you avoid actions that could put you in danger, even if the danger is imaginary. As this bubbles up to your neocortex, you're forced to generate all manner of excuses to explain your inability to take action.

Playing it safe and avoiding areas where predators might be found makes sense. It's okay if we overgeneralize in some survival situations since one mistake there could be fatal, especially during childhood. But lesser risks like embarrassment or a financial setback aren't in the same ballpark as genuine threats, even though they can trigger similar responses in your thoughts and behaviors. You can afford to endure some failure in your work and financial life for the sake of learning and growth; in fact, it's quite beneficial to do so.

Like it or not, you're still a mammal, and so you've inherited some of that mammalian mental baggage. On the bright side, you owe this part a lot of credit for enabling you to exist in the first place. On the other hand, you'll need to compensate for this baggage, assuming you'd like to live a richer life than most other mammals.

Conscious Thinking vs. Unconscious Beliefs

You have a few basic options for dealing with unconscious limiting beliefs.

Your first option is to ignore them. Let these mental subroutines continue to run as they will. If you do this, you'll most likely live an okay and mostly average life, assuming your limiting beliefs aren't too extreme. You won't get anywhere close to your potential as a conscious human being, but you can still be a proud and worthy mammal. If it's okay to continue your life on pretty much the same terms as you've been living it, then there's no real mandate to deal with your limiting beliefs. They'll exert a lot of control over how your life turns out, but if you don't mind experiencing more of the same, that's your choice to make. This is essentially the same as accepting that your past programming is the real you.

Your second option is to try to overpower your limiting beliefs. You can attempt to use your force of will to resist by pushing yourself to take action again and again. You may put systems in place to force yourself to get moving and keep moving, such as by increasing the negative consequences of quitting. This can be done, but the effects are usually very short-lived, and it can be mentally exhausting to keep it up. This strategy essentially means that one part of your brain is fighting another.

The third option is to dissolve your limiting beliefs. Instead of resisting them, you can release them. By dissolving a limiting belief, you can remove it permanently so that it no longer subconsciously affects your thinking. Essentially this means that you're deleting the old subroutines that got installed in early childhood since as an adult, you no longer need them. In place of the old beliefs, you could try to install new ones, but you could also leave the slate blank and allow your brain's own logical thinking to fill in the gap.

As an adult you no longer need childhood beliefs to keep you safe. You can use your fully developed neocortex to make more intelligent decisions. You can base your decisions on your knowledge, life experience, skills, and outcome predictions. These mental skills were less developed when you were a child, and so you needed your limbic brain to protect you. But in adulthood you can use your life experience and knowledge to determine that lions may still be dangerous while public speaking generally isn't.

It would be terrific if our brains automatically did this garbage collection as we got older. To some extent they do, but it seems to be a very gradual process. We also tend to become less emotional as we age, which can reduce the effects of childhood conditioning. But we can still speed this process along by doing some manual garbage collection to clear out the clutter of limiting beliefs that we no longer need. I really think it's wise to do this, especially during our 20s and 30s, so these beliefs don't restrict the kinds of goals we can set and accomplish in life.

Dissolving Limiting Beliefs

I could walk you through the steps to dissolve a limiting belief, but Morty Lefkoe has already put that process online, so it's easiest to simply refer you to there since you can test it for free. You'll understand it best if you experience it first-hand, and you gain the side benefit of eliminating one of your own limiting beliefs for good.

If you suspect you have limiting beliefs that are holding

you back, especially with respect to our passive income series, Morty's process will help you identify and dissolve them. For each belief, the process takes about 20 minutes, and all you really need to do is watch a video.

In less than 24 hours, I'm heading to the airport for another travel adventure, and I probably won't be blogging much while I'm gone. When I get back, I'll be just about ready to begin the walkthrough of creating a new passive income stream from scratch.

While I'm away, this would be a good time to get those pesky limiting beliefs out of your way, so you don't have to worry about them coming back to haunt you later. Then if you wish to follow along in creating your own new stream of income while I blog about creating mine, you won't be fighting yourself in your own mind. You can simply flow along with the action steps as I do them myself.

Also think of how nice it will be to go off on your own travel adventures with all your trip expenses covered by your income streams, so that you continue to earn just as much income while you're away. No need to ask anyone's approval or permission — you can just go. Remember that this isn't some crazy fantasy. If you can dissolve those limiting beliefs that are getting in your way and get into the flow of action, this is all very doable. Just don't tell your boss what you're up to.

Chapter 21

How to Earn Passive Income from Live Performance Art

Recently I attended the Winnipeg Fringe Festival, which is a festival of theatrical shows. This one included 30 venues with rotating shows running 12 hours per day. I managed to see 25 plays in 5 days, including musicals, comedies, murder mysteries, clown shows, acrobatics, performance poetry, and more. I was very impressed with the talent of the various performers, who obviously worked hard to hone their skills.

While watching some of these shows, I pondered the ephemeral nature of each performance. For an hour or two, we enjoy a delightful experience together, and then it ends. While the same play can be performed repeatedly, no two performances are quite the same. Once a show is over, it's gone forever, never to be seen again. This makes live theater a special and unique thing to behold.

Making Money from Performance Art

Consider how the actors in these plays make money. Suppose a play gets 100 people attending each performance, and suppose the troupe averages about $8 per audience member per performance in take-home pay. That's $800 per performance. With 7 performances per show at a festival, that means a troupe can earn over $5K for a 10-day festival. Some performers also generate income from back of the room sales after their shows with CDs, T-shirts, etc. A very popular show that sells out can take in $20K during a single festival.

For a one-person show, the sole performer gets the full amount, but for larger troupes this may be divided into many slices. Solo shows often sell out if the show is really good, so it's possible to earn over $100K per year by doing theatrical festivals in different cities for a few months each year. I doubt most Fringe performers earn that much, but those who are really dedicated can certainly do so.

Whether there are 10 people or 200 people in the audience, the actors must work just as hard. Their income depends not on the time they invest in each performance but on the number of people who pay to see them. If they can get 10x as many people into the seats, they'll earn 10x as much money for the same amount of stage time.

Many factors can affect the audience size, such as the show's day and time, the venue, the troupe's reputation, the subject matter, the type of show, the show's marketing, critics' reviews, attendee reviews, word of mouth, and sometimes sheer luck.

Pseudo-Passive Income

While a performer or troupe may earn a healthy hourly rate for the time on stage, of course it's the prep work that makes this possible. Many hours may be invested in creating and fine-tuning a show, but a good show can be performed dozens, if not hundreds, of times — in different cities, to different audiences, and at different times.

This level of thinking puts us somewhere in the gray area between active and passive income. To perform a show the 41st time after it's already been performed the first 40 times takes much less effort than creating the first show from scratch. The income for each incremental performance is high because it leverages creative work that's already finished, but this income stream isn't fully passive because the income stops when the show isn't being actively performed.

If you do work that involves one-time performances, realize that these are the least efficient in terms of your return on investment. Think of how you could repeat these performances multiple times to do a better job of leveraging your up-front creative efforts.

If you spend 20 hours writing and rehearsing a one-hour speech, and you deliver it only once for $2500, you'll have earned $119 per working hour. But if you can deliver that same speech 10 times for the same fee, your hourly rate will increase to $833. In the latter situation, you're still earning income actively, but you're leveraging the power of passive value to earn multiples of what you'd otherwise be paid.

How can you create something once and perform, share, or deliver it multiple times?

Passive Income from Performance Art

To make your creative work even more passive, put it into a permanent form, such that it can provide value to people even when you aren't working.

For example, record your performance or presentation, and charge for people to access it. Even if you charge much less for a recording than for a live performance, you can offer the recording to many more people. With your live performances, you may reach thousands of people, but if you can record your work, you could potentially reach tens of thousands, hundreds of thousands, or even millions of people.

If you create a live show and refine it through your own performances, and you can license your script for other troupes to perform. If you won't be performing your creative work in certain cities or countries, or if you're going to stop performing it in the future, why not allow others to perform your work as they pay you for the privilege? Some troupes are glad to perform others' work; this saves them the trouble of creating an original show from scratch and allows them to offer a show that's already proven to draw audiences. By licensing your work to other performers, new audiences can enjoy your creations that otherwise would have missed out entirely, and you can enjoy extra income without having to perform at all.

One show I saw at the Fringe Festival was called "Almost an Evening." This was a collection of plays written by Ethan Coen (of the Coen brothers, creators of *Fargo and O Brother, Where Art Thou?*). These plays were hysterically funny, and the performers did an outstanding job, especially with their rendition of dueling Old Testament and New Testament gods. Since Ethan Coen made his creative work available to this troupe to perform, he enabled hundreds of others to enjoy it in the form of a live performance.

Putting certain creations into digital form can pay off handsomely, but not every creative work lends itself well to digital media. Live theater is a one example. Watching a video of a play simply cannot provide the same you-had-to-be-there moments as you experience when sitting in the audience, especially if you have front row seats or if the show involves audience interaction. In one show with the Pi Clowns, for instance, Rachelle and I were sitting in the front row, and about halfway through the show, I was unexpectedly pulled onto the stage and invited to perform silly feats with another audience member for several minutes. That made the experience very memorable, and it guarantees that each performance will be unique, but of course this doesn't happen while watching videos at home.

If you don't feel you can put your creative work into digital form and maintain the same quality of experience, don't automatically rule out passive income. You can still generate passive income by making your work available for others to perform and charging a license fee, and you can do this more than once if you use a nonexclusive license. Others won't perform your shows, sing your songs, or deliver your presentations the same way you would, but much can be gained by allowing them to put their own spin on your work. They may even improve upon it in ways you didn't expect.

For a quality live experience, it may be true that the audience has to be there, but the creative mind that developed the work may be able to stay home or perhaps he may choose to go white water rafting in Canada such as I'm doing this week.

Chapter 22

Passive Income Walkthrough

I think we've all waited long enough. Let's begin the walk-through of creating a new stream of passive income from start to finish.

The process of creating new income streams is different for everyone, so you won't necessarily want to model my approach exactly because your knowledge, skills, and resources may not align with mine. Even so, I'm sure you'll learn something from this walkthrough.

So let's dive right in and get started.

Pick an Idea

Your first step is to pick an idea. Hopefully this is fairly obvious.

One of the simplest ways is to grab a pen and paper, and brainstorm a list of ideas. Keep writing down ideas until you run out of ideas. Then look over your list, and pick one that seems decent.

If you need help generating ideas, read the chapter "Generating Ideas" for some advice on how to do it.

Many people get caught up trying to pick an idea. If you get stuck here, you can't progress. So whatever you do, don't let yourself get stuck here. Make a decision no matter what.

One of my favorite ways to choose among different options is simply to ask, which *option is the most me?* That usually narrows it down quite a bit.

Worst case if you can't decide, flip a coin or roll a die and let chance decide. You're better off getting into action quickly than suffering useless delay and self doubt. You'll progress much faster by getting a few projects under your belt than you will be trying to dream up the perfect idea in advance. Some creative people will advise you to *fail faster*, which is good advice.

Notice that picking an idea is not the same thing as whining about why you can't pick one.

It's also not the same as saying you don't have any good ideas.

And of course it's not the same as saying "I don't know how" when you think about your favorite idea.

The truth is that good income-generating ideas are a dime a dozen. Coming up with ideas is the easy part. If you've been stuck in the corporate world for too long, then perhaps your creative impulses have been squashed to make you a better slave, so if that's the case, then go ask a nearby child what you can do to make the world better for people, and listen to what s/he has to say.

Now if you're really and truly stuck and can't come up with a decent idea, then I'd be delighted to pick one for you and assign it to you, but you may not like it unless you're Canadian and very submissive (just kidding).

My initial idea was to create some kind of digital product

and sell it. That seems simple and straightforward, and it's an approach other people can model if they so desire. I can sell something through my own website, and other people can sell digital products through Amazon, iTunes, and other online stores, depending on the format.

Refine the Idea

Depending on the nature of your idea, you may have some details to decide next.

For my product idea, I need to determine a topic and a format.

Once again, you can brainstorm possibilities. Then pick something, and keep moving forward.

Don't get caught up in vacillating. Just decide. Your decision won't be perfect, and it doesn't have to be. Just pick an idea that seems pretty good, and run with it. You'll get better at picking ideas once you've completed a few projects and saw how they turned out.

For the format I decided to create an ebook and an audio program, so I'll actually have two different products in different formats, but the underlying content will be the same. I might sell them separately or as a bundle or both, but I can decide that later.

For the topic I settled on Subjective Reality.

Why SR? For starters people have been clamoring for a more in-depth product on that for years. We had the Subjective Reality Workshop in 2011, but not everyone can make it to a 3-day workshop.

I also think this would be a fun and interesting product to create. Based on what I've seen, there isn't a lot of quality material available on SR. Most of it is either very shallow or very woo woo, and it fails to explain why we seem to have the various limitations and constraints that we do.

I doubt that SR is the topic that would make me the most money. It's a niche topic, and many people don't care to learn about it. But for those who do care, they tend to care a lot. So this is the kind of product that should have strong appeal to a certain core audience, and beyond that most people will just think it's weird. For whatever reason, this sort of product really appeals to me. I'd rather make some people really happy than lots of people only moderately happy.

So I'm choosing this topic because I think I'd enjoy it, I think enough people would appreciate it, and it's an area where I feel I can contribute something unique and worthwhile.

SR is also a timeless topic, so this product could easily sell for many years to come.

Fall in Love with Your Idea

The next step is to fall in love with your idea.

A mistake people often make is that they look to their ideas to give them confidence, as if an idea itself can provide that. In reality almost all ideas are going to feel fuzzy and uncertain at first. It's your job to inject them with confidence.

Your relationship to your idea will largely determine how far you get with it, and this relationship is under your control to a great extent.

Where does your relationship with another person exist? In your mind. Where does your relationship with an idea exist? In your mind.

If you start thinking ill about your relationship partner and succumb to doubt about your future together, what does that do to your relationship? It kills it. On the contrary, if you hold lovey dovey thoughts towards your relationship partner, does that not improve the relationship? Of course.

With an idea it's even easier. Treat your idea as if it's the most amazing thing ever. Respect it. Honor it. Fall head over heels in love with it.

Don't look to your idea to provide you with inspiration and motivation. Don't try to suck your idea dry like you're sucking an orange. You must let the inspiration flow the other way. You must feed and water and nurture your idea, helping to give it form and substance. You're the creative conduit here, not the idea.

If you don't fall in love with it, why would you expect anyone else to? An unloved idea will lead to a crappy result that no one will want.

Have fun with this. Be playful about it.

By way of example, I'm making myself fall in love with my subjective reality product. It's going to be the coolest, deepest, and most mind-blowing product on the topic that anyone has ever seen.

Who cares if that's actually true? It's fun and motivating to inject your idea with positive expectations. Self-doubt is only going to slow things down, so don't even go there.

Once you've selected your idea, the evaluation period is over. Like a newborn child, you've named it and claimed it and taken it home with you. It's too late to decide whether or not it's a good idea. It's yours now, and you'd better learn to love it.

Devise an Income Stream for Your Idea

Some ideas are easy to adapt to income streams. Others require a bit more finesse.

In the case of an ebook and audio program, my intention is to package these as digitally downloadable products and sell them directly via my website.

Later I may sell them through other sites like Amazon, but for the purposes of this demonstration, I want to keep it simple.

What if you don't have a high-traffic website like I do? Then you're not likely to generate many sales if all you do is post it on your website.

When I released computer games before I had much web traffic, I spent a lot of time marketing them. Basically this involved uploading the free demos to hundreds of download sites, buying some online ads, sending out press releases, and more. For one game I spent about 6 months marketing it after it was released. This made a big difference, increasing the sales by 10 times.

If you've fallen in love with your idea, you'll have a lot of motivation to do this part. But if you don't love it, I'd bet money that you'll drop the ball here.

I see a lot of would-be online entrepreneurs create and release products they clearly don't love. They'll usually spread the word for a few weeks, and then they give up and let the income stream die. People can tell it's a me-too product, so they don't buy. With an unloved product, this is enough discouragement to call it quits. With a product you really love, however, you'll be able to push through and keep putting the word out.

It's not enough to just create a cool product and hope people will buy it. You have to let people know about it. Once you build enough momentum, your sales may become self-sustaining, but don't assume this will happen automatically just because you created something and put it on the Internet.

In my case I own some marketing vehicles that I can use, like my website and newsletter. I can also use my Twitter and Google+ accounts to get the word out. Blogging about the development of this product along the way can also be seen as a way of marketing it. Many people who are following the passive income series won't care about an SR product, but some will. So there will probably be some decent interest in the product when it launches.

I can share more ideas about marketing later in the series. For now, let me just say that you can expect to spend as least as much time marketing your new product or service as you do creating it. If you don't love your creation, that's a headache. If you love it, then getting the word out won't be so bad.

The good news is that you don't need to design your own income-generating process from scratch. I'm certainly not doing that here. You can borrow someone else's fully developed system, such as the ones I shared earlier.

Outline the Idea

Your next step is to outline the idea. What do you think you'll include?

For my SR product, I came up with a rough chapter outline:

Part I – Understanding Subjective Reality

1. Introduction

2. What Is SR?

3. Lucid Dreaming

4. SR. vs. OR / Equivalency Principle

5. Understanding Beliefs / Observing or Causing Reality

6. Changing Beliefs

7. Living Subjectively

Part II – Applying Subjective Reality

1. The Law of Attraction

2. Creating Your Reality

3. Subjective Reality and Money

4. Subjective Relationships

Part III – Integrating Subjective Reality

1. Merging Subjectivity and Objectivity

2. Reality as Story

3. Final Wisdom / Closing

Now this is only a rough draft, not necessarily the final outline of the completed product, but it gets me started and helps me see what I want to include. For example, I know I'm going to cover the Law of Attraction in this product.

The idea is to create something to help guide you in your development process, but don't let this part bog you down. If you're spending more than an hour on it, I think that's too long. Just aim for something that looks halfway decent. If you can't manage halfway decent, then settle for indecent. You can always change it later.

It's pretty easy to get stuck in this stage, so that's why I like to move through it quickly. If you're building a space rocket or a hospital, then it makes sense to invest in careful planning. But for a flexible digital product, overplanning tends to be a much greater risk. We just need a general idea of the main sections, so we can start filling in the content.

Create a Simple Completion Plan

Now that we have an idea and a rough outline, how are we going to get this done?

The previous steps in this article are pretty straightforward. You can do them in less than an hour. If it takes longer than that, you're probably getting stuck in vacillating. Just make a decision at each step and move on.

Lots of interesting ideas die somewhere between here and full completion. So let's pay some attention to how you're going to complete this and get it done.

For one-person projects like this, it doesn't make sense to get bogged down in overplanning. Some people spend more time planning a project and getting ready to begin, when it would have taken less time to just dive in and do it.

I favor the dive in and do it approach, which has worked beautifully for blogging, but since this is a larger work, I want to make sure I have a process that I trust will converge on a completed product.

Here's my basic action plan to move this project forward to completion:

1. Each day until the ebook is complete, I'll create a minimum of 5,000 words of fresh content, and this will be edited content of publishable quality. This includes weekends.

2. I'll keep adding 5,000 or more words of content to the product until I'm satisfied that the content is complete.

3. For each section I'll jot down some quick notes for the key points, stories, and examples I intend to include. Then I'll use the built-in dictation on my MacBook Pro (dictation is part of OS X Mountain Lion) to speak the content aloud into a Pages document. If I don't like this process or if the dictation quality isn't good enough, then I'll fall back on just typing the content like I do with blog articles.

4. After I dictate a section of content, I'll do an editing pass to correct errors, add subsection headers, and improve coherence and flow.

5. At the end of each day, I'll bring all of the existing content to a publishable level of quality, meaning that it would meet my standards for something I could publish to my blog. This is an important lesson I learned from writing software — always bring the code to a publishable level of quality at the end of each day. Fix mistakes and low quality work as soon as possible since it takes much longer to fix them later.

6. Once I have the first draft done, I'll give it another editing pass and have a few others check it for typos and mistakes. I may keep doing rounds of this till I'm satisfied we've got the final content good to go.

7. Once the ebook content is done, I'll have someone who's more aesthetically minded format it to look nice, including creating a cover page.

8. After the ebook is complete, I'll use it as the script to record the audio program. Since the initial content will have been spoken for dictation, it should make for a natural sounding script for the audio. I may not record it word for word exactly, but the core content will be the same. I think this will yield a more polished audio program than if I try to use the initial, unedited dictation sessions. I'll probably use the same recording equipment I used for podcasting.

9. I'll have someone help me edit the audio files, add intro music, turn them into MP3s, and help package the results into a completed audio program.

10. Once these products are complete, I'll create a sales page for them, add them to the online shopping cart, add links through my website, and announce them on my blog, newsletter, and Twitter and Google+ pages.

So that's the basic plan.

Now all sorts of things could go wrong with this plan. Maybe maintaining 5K words per day will be too much. Maybe I'll need to take weekends off to regain my sanity. Maybe the Mac dictation won't be good enough, and I'll have to fall back on typing all the content. That's okay. The plan can always be adapted as needed. The point of planning is to envision a path to completion. What I have above looks good enough to me.

I also have some travel coming up, so I'll need to work around that. The first trip is less than 3 weeks away, and I'll be gone for nearly 2 weeks. Then I'll be back for a few days, and

I have another short trip after that. It's doubtful I'll want to keep working on this while I'm on the road, so in that case I'll probably put this work on pause and continue where I left off when I return. Travel is a big part of my lifestyle, so I'm fine having this project take a bit longer to work around these trips.

I know that if I hit a certain content quota each day, and if I bring the existing content to publishable quality at the end of each day, I'll eventually have a completed ebook. And using that to record an audio version should be pretty straightforward. So even with some travel breaking things up, this will eventually converge as long as I stick with it.

How long will this product be? I don't know maybe 60-100K words (6-10 hours of audio), but it could be a lot more. I'll create as much as it takes to do the topic justice and feel satisfied with the end result. The length doesn't really matter since it's going to be digital. I'm not planning to make print books or CDs since physical media is all but obsolete. If some people won't buy it because it's digital only, I'm perfectly okay with that. Most of my website visitors are under age 30, and past surveys showed that most of them prefer digital products anyway. Less than 2% said they wouldn't buy something with no physical media, and dealing with physical media isn't worth it to capture an extra 2%.

Price-wise I'm leaning towards $15 for the ebook, $15 for the audio, and $25 for both together. I think that's very reasonable, especially for a niche product. I'm sure I could sell this for more, but I don't want people who want it to feel that the price is a barrier for them.

My initial intention, which I shared earlier in this series, was to create a new income stream of $2K or more per month that lasts for 10 years minimum. If the average sale is $20,

I'd have to sell 100 copies per month, which is just over 3 copies per day. For all the outlets I have available, I think that's an achievable goal.

What Are Your Passive Income Priorities?

There are lots of ways to set up an income stream, so let me caution you to be careful what you optimize for.

Many people try to maximize income or profits, but this often involves sacrificing other things in exchange for more money, such as your ability to communicate as a real human being. For instance, you may need to be a lot pushier and more aggressive with your selling process if you want to squeeze more money out of people who are on the fence about buying. To me this is a big turnoff.

My motivation is to do something creative that I'll enjoy, to contribute something of value to people's lives, and to share it in such a way that some financial support flows back to me. For me a homerun is what I do on the creative side.

Another important factor for me is to avoid creating headaches for myself. I really don't care about fighting piracy, so if people want to steal a copy without paying for it, that's their choice. I don't think $15 or $25 is too much to ask for a cool and interesting product like this.

As for whether or not to keep this product copyrighted or make it un-copyrighted, I decided to keep it copyrighted, at least initially. All my blog posts are un-copyrighted, but for a product such as this, I'd rather keep ownership of the copyright. This intuitively feels right to me. I can always un-copyright it later if I so choose, but once I do that, it's irreversible. I'm still observing the ongoing ripples of un-copyrighting my articles, so I want more time to see how that turns out. It's only been a couple of years so far.

During the past 8 years, I've given away a lot of content for free. The payment I ask in return is that I'm allowed to enjoy my life — to be happy and fulfilled in living how I wish to live. I like creating passive income streams because they make it easier to center my life around learning, exploring, connecting, and sharing.

Your priorities may be different than mine, so it makes sense to adapt your passive income stream to suit your own desires. Just don't assume that maximizing income is necessarily the best approach for you. It's not an approach I'd be happy with.

Your Turn

If you're going to follow along with your own idea, then I encourage you to pick an idea, create a quick outline, and determine how you're going to move it forward to completion. There's no time like the present!

Please don't feel pressured to follow me in real time with the creation of your own income stream. I obviously have some advantages and experience that many others don't. Feel free to work through this walkthrough at whatever pacing works for you.

Incidentally, this summer was my 20-year anniversary of not having a job. That's 20 continuous years of unemployment. Booyah!

www.ingramcontent.com/pod-product-compliance
Lightning Source LLC
LaVergne TN
LVHW021450080426
835509LV00018B/2225